"If you don't want to make th⟨⟩ ⟨⟩his book. But if you're ready to tal⟨⟩ ⟨⟩n. Becky's powerful message wi⟨⟩ ⟨⟩ld change often begins with the smallest acts of love. And each of us can change the world right where we are."

—**Alicia Bruxvoort**, Proverbs 31 Ministries writer, speaker, and abundant-life seeker

"Becky's timely book is a healing balm for a broken world and a cynical heart. The stories and practical applications have been forged in her life and leadership among our faith community. This book is sure to encourage you to love generously and discover God's redemptive purposes."

—**Judy Episcopo**, women's ministry director, Appleton Alliance Church, Wisconsin

"Encouraging and practical, *Generous Love* is the perfect how-to guide for loving well in day-to-day life. Becky's words and stories highlight the powerful impact made by even the smallest acts of kindness, and her insight leaves me feeling both equipped and inspired."

—**Jen Weaver**, author of A *Wife's Secret to Happiness*

"I want to get this dynamic book into the hands of every single person I know. Becky Kopitzke is taking us back to the basics of loving others well, which in turn revolutionizes the world with the love of Christ. She reminds us that loving others doesn't have to be hard or dependent upon complicated gestures. Rather, it is the simple things such as looking each other in the eye, gifting a heartfelt compliment, and saying thank you. I am certain *Generous Love* will take the world by storm as readers apply its biblical, practical, and fun wisdom."

—**Sarah Philpott, PhD**, author of *Loved Baby: 31 Devotions Helping You Grieve and Cherish Your Child After Pregnancy Loss*

generous love

generous love

Discover the Joy
of Living
"Others First"

Becky Kopitzke

BETHANYHOUSE
a division of Baker Publishing Group
Minneapolis, Minnesota

© 2018 by Becky Kopitzke

Published by Bethany House Publishers
11400 Hampshire Avenue South
Bloomington, Minnesota 55438
www.bethanyhouse.com

Bethany House Publishers is a division of
Baker Publishing Group, Grand Rapids, Michigan

Printed in the United States of America

ISBN 978-0-7642-3053-0

Library of Congress Control Number: 2017961596

18 19 20 21 22 23 24   7 6 5 4 3 2 1

For the Stoffels

Contents

Contents

It Starts with One

We sat at her dining table, stabbing plastic forks into Chinese take-out. My sweet friend spoke gently—about her health, her spirit, her sleepless nights. I listened, nodded, and let my heart swell with each word.

We had just spent the morning on the second floor of Erin's home, organizing clutter and assembling new shelves for her children's bedrooms. We rearranged picture books and collected a small pile of stray Legos that had been left stranded under beds and on dressers. Simple chores, really, but important steps toward creating a fresh space for this beautiful family in this house that held a presence so thick you could feel it prickling on your skin.

Earlier that morning, I had arrived at her back door with two lattes in my hands, and she led me upstairs to a closet. "I forgot about this one," she said, then opened the door to reveal a small space packed tight with cardboard boxes and a row of men's shirts on hangers. In a moment my brain registered the scene, and a gasp of breath caught in my throat.

These were her husband's shirts.

Jon.

Gone, eight months ago, into the arms of Jesus.

And I tried not to let her see my eyes fill with tears.

Quickly, I grabbed a Rubbermaid bin and set to work. She pulled shirts from the closet, and I folded them into neat stacks. *This one was from high school. That one he wore to work. How long has he had these overalls, anyway? Now, this sweatshirt—there's a story behind this one.*

We chatted and folded and cleaned out that closet until it became clear we had more stuff than space to put it. "I don't think we're going to fit all these," I said—and then I volunteered to run to Walmart to buy a few more bins, mostly out of a heart to serve, but also, I confess, so I could let the tears leak down my cheeks as I drove to the store to call my own husband just to hear his voice.

Now, a few hours later, after a job well done, we were rewarding ourselves with fried rice and Hunan shrimp, talking softly across the lunch table about God's grace even in the midst of grief.

"The last year of our marriage was the best one," Erin told me.

"Really?" I smiled, encouraging the happy memories. "Why do you say that?"

"We just treated each other differently—really listening and putting each other first. We were more intentional about our actions toward each other," she explained. "I would do something to bless him, then he would do something to bless me. . . . It was like we couldn't wait to *outbless* each other."

Outbless.

The word stunned me in my seat. I blinked and let it soak deep, and I knew at that moment God was speaking to my heart. Erin continued her story.

"It really starts with yourself. I stopped looking for Jon to fulfill my needs because I knew he couldn't do that. Only God could. So I asked God for wisdom as a wife. I grew to know Jon's needs and what made him happy. To not get upset with the little things that bugged me. We started communicating better, too, talking about our feelings and encouraging each other. I knew he needed to be told he was appreciated and that all he has done for our family has not gone unnoticed. As I wanted to bless Jon more, it came back full circle. He did the same. We grew so much that year in our marriage and began to see real change in each of our hearts. Our love just grew."

Erin started giving Jon more snuggles and hugs, even though outward affection didn't come naturally to her. He, in turn, became more attentive and helpful around the house. She cooked his favorite venison steak. He fixed the sink. She held his hand. He prayed for her.

And so it continued for an entire year, blessing spurring blessing, husband to wife and wife to husband, until one memorable day when a trip to a wedding demonstrated how deep her husband's tenderness had grown.

Jon was a groomsman and a well-loved extrovert. Erin had no ties to the wedding party and knew none of the other guests. It was the kind of situation in which my soft-spoken friend would normally blend into the background and fend for herself while her hubby bounced from table to table, socializing and enjoying the party.

But not that night.

"He went out of his way to make sure I was okay," she told me. "Did I need anything? Was I having fun? Could he get me another soda? Would I like to dance? His attention really touched me."

So on the drive home she thanked him—for stepping outside of himself and showering her with extra care. She *acknowledged his blessing* and felt compelled to return it, just as she had done all year long.

Two weeks later, Jon was killed in a random shooting at a local park, a tragedy that also claimed the life of their eldest daughter. It was a horrific event that stunned our community and stirred thousands of people to tears and prayer. The last words Erin heard Jon say—as they both lay critically wounded and their two younger children ran for help—sparked a nationwide media buzz in the days to follow.

He spoke directly to the shooter.

"May God forgive you."

How is such forgiveness possible? How could those words be the final plea of a dying man's heart? How did Erin endure such grief and physical pain yet continue to breathe in, breathe out, and wake each day testifying to the goodness of God? How does she still?

There is only one answer.

Love.

> We love because he first loved us.
>
> 1 John 4:19

That kind of tremendous selflessness and hope is only possible through the supernatural love of our Father. And we, as mere mortals, have access to that love, to receive it, pass it on, and thereby revolutionize a dark and messed-up world with glimpses of heavenly light.

> You are the light of the world. A town built on a hill cannot be hidden. Neither do people light a lamp and put it under a bowl. Instead they put it on its stand, and it gives light to everyone in the house. In the same way, let your light shine before others, that they may see your good deeds and glorify your Father in heaven.
>
> Matthew 5:14–16

What is a shining light? In a word, it's a *blessing*. Love in motion. And *love*? Well, that's what distinguishes Christ's people from the rest of the world.

> Your love for one another will prove to the world that you are my disciples.
>
> John 13:35 NLT

Since that lunchtime conversation, I've spent countless hours exploring this concept. Generous love is more than a singular act of kindness or an isolated whim of generosity. It's a habit. A lifestyle. A default choice.

It's an uprising in the making.

Just imagine!

What would the world look like if we all made intentional efforts to bless one another? If in our key relationships—spouse, children, friends, church—we thought less of "self" and more of "others" and then committed to making the first move?

No more waiting for your husband to pick up his dirty socks off the bedroom floor. The wife who loves generously will pick them up herself and throw them in the wash. Crazy, right? But that's not all. Perhaps she will even match them when they're clean—and go so far as to put them away in her husband's drawer just because she knows he needs fresh socks to wear to work this week. No hint of resentment. No grumbling.

No joke.

And the husband who loves his wife will recognize she's had a long, exhausting day. So he'll pull out the kettle and boil her favorite pasta for dinner—without being asked. Maybe—*madness!*—he'll even scrub the dishes when dinner is done.

For real.

Then the woman whose agenda is packed tight this week will read on Facebook that her neighbor's son just had his tonsils taken out. So she'll invest an extra ten minutes while running her endless errands to pick up a box of cherry Popsicles and drop them off next door.

It's not so hard, is it? The actions themselves are simple, really. And yet achieving them requires chiseling away our hardened shells of pride, entitlement, and self-absorption. It calls for a total abolition of arrogance and stinginess. It begs us to open our eyes and look outward, not just inward. And that might be one of the most difficult endeavors any sinful human being can face.

Yet it's exponentially worthwhile.

In the pages to follow, we will discover the what, why, and how of *loving others* through generous blessings. What is a blessing? What does the Bible say, and why should we care? What are some practical ways to bless the people God gave us—our family, our friends, our church, and our community? Together we'll transform our focus on self into a heart for others, for the sake of strengthening *us*. Are you excited? I sure am.

Just like Erin's best year of marriage started with a single blessing, that's how it begins for you and me, too. One blessing sparks another blessing, which sparks another and another until our lives are characterized by perpetual blessings upon blessings, love reaching forward to touch the people around us. And we will discover we really can revolutionize the world with the love of Christ—one blessing at a time.

> We have all benefited from the rich blessings he brought to us— blessing upon blessing heaped upon us!
>
> John 1:16 TLB

— Chapter 1 —

What Is a Blessing, Anyway?

I heard sharp gulps of breath, three in a row, and I braced myself for the blow.

"*Ah-chooo!*" My daughter tucked her nose into her elbow and sneezed.

"Bless you," I said.

"Thanks, Mom." She tilted her head toward me and wrinkled her eyebrows. "Why do people say 'bless you' after somebody sneezes?"

Huh. Good question.

"I'm not sure, sweetheart."

So we did what every modern intellect does in a quandary. We Googled it.

Apparently ancient folklore says a sneeze was once believed to be the body's way of ridding evil spirits.[1] Creepy, eh?

Centuries later a sneeze was considered a sign that a person had contracted the plague. Ouch. In which case, "God bless you" wasn't so much a friendly salutation but rather a farewell kiss.

Even in today's age of dust allergies and antibiotics, "bless you" is still the knee-jerk response to a sneeze. Try *ah-choo*ing in the middle of a meeting and you're bound to hear a few *gesundheits* tossed your way.

But is that all a blessing is, really? Surely it's more than a casual wish for God to protect your sinuses. When someone asks "How are you?" what do you say? When life is going well, when everybody's happy and healthy and we've got money in the bank, we say we're good, we're great, we're blessed.

We're plenty eager to take all the blessings we can get.

Yet sadly for many of us, the only time we think about blessing another person is after they've blown a trajectory of germs across the room.

What does it mean to give and receive a blessing? What power does a blessing hold? Those questions are the foundation of our journey over these next sixteen chapters. And the answers begin with the first story ever told.

On the Fifth Day, God Created the Blessing

Did you know God created the blessing even before He created the first human being? It's true.

> And God said, "Let the water teem with living creatures, and let birds fly above the earth across the vault of the sky." So God created the great creatures of the sea and every living thing with which the water teems and that moves about in it, according to their kinds, and every winged bird according to its kind. And God saw that it was good. *God blessed them* and said, "Be fruitful and increase in number and fill the water in the seas, and let the birds increase on the earth."
>
> Genesis 1:20–22, emphasis added

In Bible history, Adam and Eve were created on the sixth day. But first, God spent a workweek creating their dwelling place—land and sea, plants and trees, light and dark, animals that swam and flew and ran. And when God looked around at all He had formed by the end of the fifth day—before man arrived to mess it up—He saw it was pretty awesome. So He commanded the fish and birds to multiply, to be fruitful, to *make more awesomeness.*

This was called a blessing.

Later, God gave a similar blessing to Adam and Eve: "God blessed them and said to them, 'Be fruitful and increase in number; fill the earth and subdue it'" (Genesis 1:28). The Hebrew word for *bless* here is *barak,* which means to praise, congratulate, salute. It's the same term God used when He told Abraham to go to the promised land, where He would shower him with prosperity and welfare.

> I will make you into a great nation, and I will bless you; I will make your name great, and you will be a blessing. I will bless those who bless you, and whoever curses you I will curse; and all peoples on earth will be blessed through you.
>
> Genesis 12:2–3

Another Hebrew word for *bless* in the Bible is *esher,* which means happiness. We find this term often in the Psalms.

> Blessed [esher] is the one who does not walk in step with the wicked or stand in the way that sinners take or sit in the company of mockers, but whose delight is in the law of the Lord, and who meditates on his law day and night. That person is like a tree planted by streams of water, which yields its fruit in season and whose leaf does not wither—whatever they do prospers.
>
> Psalm 1:1–3

When we put it all together, we see that a blessing is a gift we not only receive from God but also pass on to others. To bless someone is to hold them in high esteem, to enrich their life, and to magnify their awesomeness in a way that honors God, the source of everything awesome.

We can be blessed by God and others and, like Abraham, we can also be a blessing, meaning other people can be blessed through us—all because God blessed us first.

It's a chain reaction.

I call it living "others first."

Give: Be a Blessing

My mentor, Cindy, has a motto for her relationship with her son-in-law: "Be a blessing!" When her daughter got married, Cindy resolved to be the mother-in-law who sweetens her child's marriage rather than souring it. How? By encouraging her daughter to love her husband. By supporting her son-in-law's role as head of his household. By not sticking her nose in their business when they don't ask for it. By treating her son-in-law as she treats her own sons.

I don't think I need to tell you that this kind of selfless behavior does not come naturally to every mother-in-law in the universe. Heavens, it doesn't come naturally to any of us—probably not even to Cindy, which is why she needs the motto in the first place.

To be a blessing means to bless someone else—with your words or gestures or your very presence—for the sake of showing love, respect, appreciation, and acceptance. It's putting into action an attitude of grace and generosity toward another human being—and even toward God.

Bless the Lord, O my soul, and forget not all his benefits.

Psalm 103:2 ESV

To bless God means to praise Him. To bless other people may also mean to praise them for their character or accomplishments, or to help them, support them, encourage them, equip them, affirm them, or to somehow invoke happiness in their lives.

Phew! Do you see? There are about as many ways to bless someone as there are moments in the day. But don't worry. You'll quickly get the hang of it. Later in this book we'll explore several practical ideas for blessing the people around you. Then soon enough you'll be coming up with hundreds of ideas all on your own.

Receive: Be Blessed

Likewise, when someone blesses us, we ought to feel encouraged, equipped, supported, and loved. This is what it means to be blessed.

When my husband takes my car for a spin just to fill it with gas—I am blessed.

When my friend offers to watch my children for an afternoon so I can run errands—I am blessed.

When a reader emails to say she printed one of my blog posts and refers to it daily—I am blessed indeed.

God himself blesses us every day just by holding the world in balance and watching over our every move. One of my favorite quotes is by theologian and author John Piper: "God is always doing 10,000 things in your life, and you may be aware of three of them."[2] The Lord is constantly blessing us, even when we are clueless.

As a natural outpouring of our gratitude toward God for His blessings, we ought to be motivated to bless others. And in turn, those people will be more likely to bless us back and to pay forward still more blessings to more people, and so the cycle spins on.

Sound idealistic? Like wishful thinking? Maybe. Especially since the world doesn't appear to operate on this happy system as a general rule most days. But I believe it can, if we make the first move.

Why? Because the Bible says so.

For God, who gives seed to the farmer to plant, and later on good crops to harvest and eat, will give you more and more seed to plant and will make it grow so that you can give away more and more fruit from your harvest. Yes, God will give you much so that you can give away much, and when we take your gifts to those who need them they will break out into thanksgiving and praise to God for your help.

2 Corinthians 9:10–11 TLB

Everybody Wins

In order to fully understand and implement the concept of generous love—of selflessly blessing the people in our lives—we first need to recognize what generous love is not.

It's not a competition. If your intention is to show someone up and prove you're better at blessing than they are, then your actions are rooted in selfishness, not generosity.

It's not a compromise. Blessing is not about meeting in the middle. It requires crossing over to another person's side—seeing your relationship from their point of view, and serving them according to their needs rather than your own.

It's not passive-aggression. Coating underlying anger or resentment in sweet gestures is like pouring chocolate sauce on a bowl of five-alarm chili. It doesn't hide the burn. Blessing others can be part of the remedy for healing what lies beneath, yes, but it cannot be a shroud.

It's not an ulterior motive or a hint—that the *blessee* should do something nice for you in return. Yes, hopefully your blessing will spark more blessing. But if it's delivered with the intention of giving in order to get, that's not a pure blessing, and you've missed the whole point.

A blessing is a simple act of selfless love, just because you care about another human being—or more important, because you care about God, who loves that person more than you do. It looks something like this.

And So I Washed His Coffee Mug

I had deadlines. Projects to tackle, emails to answer, phone calls to take. As soon as I walked in the house after school drop-off that morning, I gave myself exactly five minutes to load the dishwasher before parking my bottom in my desk chair for the remainder of the day.

Dishes in, table wiped, faucet off—and that's when I saw it. Sitting on the counter beside the sink, my husband's favorite Starbucks travel mug, dirty. Hand-wash only.

I could've let it sit. It was *his* mug, after all, and he didn't expect me to wash it. I don't drink coffee unless it's made by a barista, laced with oodles of chocolate, and poured into a disposable to-go cup. So in our house we have an unspoken agreement that the kitchen coffee maker, the coffee grounds, and the half-dozen ceramic mugs my husband used to leave sitting in the car week by week—which is why I bought him the travel mug in the first place—are all *his* deal. So let him scrub his own precious mug. I had other stuff to do.

But.

How long would it take me to wash that mug? Sixty seconds, tops? And I was already standing at the sink. The water was already hot. The scrub brush was just three inches from my fingertips.

Why shouldn't I wash the mug?

Better question—why *should* I?

If washing that mug says *I love you* and *I'm thinking of you* and *You matter to me*, isn't that worth a one-minute sacrifice out of my day?

Isn't it worth way more than that?

> And do not forget to do good and to share with others, for with such sacrifices God is pleased.
>
> Hebrews 13:16

Deep relationships aren't built on emotional highs. They're made strong through a bunch of little gestures that are so easily overlooked and underspent. And when we pass on those little

23

gestures day after day after day, when we get in the habit of thinking *me* instead of *you* or *us*, even the emotional highs (if we're blessed enough to get them) can't fill the cracks left by missed opportunities to express love for the people God placed in our sphere.

Yes, I had deadlines. I had a stack of to-do's waiting at my desk. But I grabbed that travel mug and scrubbed it shiny clean for the love of my life, the man God picked out of a crowd for me even before I knew who God was. He deserves my attention and my sacrifice and my willingness to serve—even when it's inconvenient—because loving him is, in essence, loving the One who gave him to me. And all it took was a travel mug to remind me of that very core truth.

So what about you? What little gesture can you make today and tomorrow and the day after that? What easily overlooked choices can you make that say *I'm on your side?* Day after day, those little choices will add up. And one day we'll look back over the years and be able to say to the people God gave us, *Our relationship is strong because I loved you in the little things. I was true to you in thought and deed.*

I washed your mug.

Because you mean the world to me.

Do you see? True blessings are given freely and without selfish motives. Totally contrary to our nature, isn't it? That's why, in our next couple chapters, we're going to dig to the root of our selfishness and pull those suffocating "me" weeds straight from the depth of our hearts, one by one.

─────── Let's Dig Deeper ───────

1. In your own words, explain what a blessing is. What does it mean to be blessed? What does it mean to bless others?

2. Think of the last time someone blessed you. What did they do? Why did it impact you?

3. Consider Cindy's motto: "Be a blessing!" To what relationships do you personally need to apply this attitude?

4. Is it difficult for you to make the first move? To bless someone even if they are not asking for your blessing? Why or why not?

5. Consider John Piper's quote: "God is always doing 10,000 things in your life, and you may be aware of three of them." How does this affect the way you look at your circumstances? What does it say about your relationship with God? (For further discussion, see Proverbs 16:9; Romans 8:28; and Job 42:2.)

6. Discuss why blessing cannot be approached as a competition. How does a competitive spirit hinder the purpose?

7. Consider this statement again: "Blessing is not about meeting in the middle. It requires crossing over to another person's side." How willing are you to step into another person's shoes? Why is "meeting in the middle" not an effective way to bless?

8. Who is ultimately blessed the most by our efforts to care for others? See Hebrews 13:16.

Love in Motion

This week, wash your husband's coffee mug (so to speak). Choose one small, out-of-the-ordinary gesture to bless someone you love. How did it make you feel? Did the other person respond? It's okay if they didn't! You're just beginning a long journey. For now the important thing is to make the first move.

— Chapter 2 —

Why Are We
So Stinking Selfish?

Once upon a time I thought I was a giving type of person. Then I got married, and I discovered how much I liked getting my own way.

I used to think I was patient and gentle, too—until I had kids. Then my patience sank into a pool of their whining and bickering.

For sure I never considered myself an angry or cynical person, until the first time someone close to me so wounded my heart that it turned bitter inside. If only I'd never gotten hurt like that, I'd be different today.

Can you relate?

In other words, *I used to be more selfless and joyful and kind.* But no longer. Because my life circumstances, my relationships, these people along my path—*they made me this way.*

Hmm. Is that so?

The Bible would argue otherwise.

But I was born a sinner, yes, from the moment my mother conceived me.

Psalm 51:5 TLB

I Was Born a What?

The ugly truth is that nobody makes us into something we're not. Our experiences, our relationships, our struggles and pain—they only reveal what was inside us all the while.

Sounds kind of harsh, right? Please understand, I know some of you have suffered deep injustice, and my heart aches for women—many of them my own dear friends—who have been victims of abuse, neglect, tragedy, or hardship. Such horrific circumstances can certainly shape us and chafe our souls raw.

But even our most awful experiences cannot create sin within us. The sin was there all along. The question is—will you allow it to pull you away from God or closer to Him?

That Dreaded S Word

What do I mean by *sin*, exactly? The word gets a bad rap among people who picture devils in red capes and pitchforks, as though calling someone a sinner is a ghastly insult. Yet it's no more insulting to call me a sinner than it is to say I have blue eyes or long legs. Sin is an inherent characteristic of my humanity and yours. It's junk like selfishness, pride, envy, greed—a whole horde of predispositions that are opposed to God. We were born with it. And that junk is what makes it so hard for us to bless other people.

For example, God says be kind. So if we snap at our kids, that's sin.

God says be honest. So if we tell a friend we're sorry we missed her call when really we purposely ignored it, that's sin. Bummer, right?

And God says don't gossip. So if we relish whispering about the co-worker who just got fired, well, that, too, is sin.

Many of us would pass off such behaviors as harmless. But the Bible says they're not. Because any sin, no matter the size or shape or intention, is offensive to God.

Feeling crummy yet? You should. But hold on. There's good news.

First of all, you're not alone. Not a single person in this world is without the junk. Romans 3:23 says, "For all have sinned and fall short of the glory of God." That doesn't make it okay, but it does make it, unfortunately, normal.

Second, sin is nothing new. It started when Adam and Eve ate the forbidden fruit, and every human being since has spent a lifetime on earth combating the junk within us. You and I are no exception. Just yesterday I told my children I was going to jump out a window if they couldn't figure out how to share the bathroom sink. I think that's called impatience. Or anger, discord, dissention, fits of rage (see Galatians 5:19–21 for more lovely options) . . . I could go on. But even I need my third point by now.

The best news is that we don't have to be stuck in our sin forever. God gave us a way out.

Jesus: The Life-Changer

We're all born with a sin nature. This inherent sin separates us from God. It creates a chasm between us and heaven. The only way to be reunited with God is to be perfect and never sin (not gonna happen), or to let somebody who *is* perfect take our place—Jesus, the Son of God.

Jesus, who was actually God in human form, came to earth two thousand years ago to live the impeccable, sin-free life that we are incapable of living, and to die the terrible death (nailed to a cross!) that we deserve because, well, we've got this sin thing.

Three days after He was buried, Jesus rose—still alive but in His pure, glorified body—back to heaven where He is now working alongside God the Father. Together they are saving a special room—in heaven!—for each of us.

There are many rooms in My Father's house. If it were not so, I would have told you. I am going away to make a place for you. After

I go and make a place for you, I will come back and take you with
Me. Then you may be where I am.

John 14:2–3 NLV

All this defies human logic. But salvation *shouldn't* make sense.
It's just that awesome.

As the heavens are higher than the earth, so are my ways higher
than your ways and my thoughts than your thoughts.

Isaiah 55:9

A Matter of the Heart

Armed with the power of God, we can begin peeling back the layers
of junk that prohibit us from blessing other people. At the core of
our sin nature is selfishness—a deeply ingrained tendency to look
out for ourselves before we tend to other people.

If you're a mother or a caregiver, you might argue you don't have
a chance to look out for yourself; all your time is spent taking care
of everybody else. I get that, sister. I've sacrificed many an hour to
poopy diapers and math homework. Our responsibilities as wives,
mothers, daughters, friends, employees, church members, and,
well, *grown-ups* can render "me time" an elusive luxury. We'll talk
more about that in chapter 4.

Selfishness does not discriminate according to age or stage or
circumstance, because selfishness is not only about how we spend
our time or who demands our attention. If devoting days on end
to someone else's needs is all it takes to be selfless, then toss me a
sash because I'm the Queen of the Selfless Pageant by now.

Selfishness is an issue of the heart. I could easily spend a day at
the office, or volunteering at church, or chaperoning a field trip,
and resent it all the while. Because what if what I really wanted to do
that day was go shopping or work on a writing project or sleep? And
my job, my ministry, that field trip—they kept me from my wants.

The Most Important Choice You'll Ever Make

Do you want to claim your room in heaven? (Some Bible translations actually call it a "mansion." Woot!) Here's how I did it, and you can do it, too. In modern Christian-speak, it's called "putting Jesus in the driver's seat" or choosing "new life." And yes, it is a *choice*—the most important one you'll ever make. Salvation does not happen by default. You're not born into it as a child; salvation is not in your genes or your religious upbringing. It does not come through osmosis simply by showing up at church or reading Bible studies. It's a personal decision you make—at some critical point—to place Jesus in charge of your life. For me, it began with a prayer.

Lord, I've messed up. I sin every day, even in ways I don't realize. Will you please forgive me? I don't want to be separated from you anymore. I don't want to be a slave to sin. I want you to run my life and show me how to obey you and love you. Please take over, Jesus. I need you.

If you pray a prayer like that and mean it, three things happen:

- You're choosing to follow Jesus and to trust that what He wants for you is what's best for you. The Bible is filled with the hows and whys of living for Christ. It'll take you a lifetime to figure it out. Enjoy the ride.

- You're inviting Jesus to take your place when you die and stand before God the Father. He'll look at you and see Jesus, His perfect, unblemished Son—which means you are now qualified to take up eternal residence in your fancy new room (i.e., mansion).

- You don't have to sin anymore. Oh, you will, believe me—but sin is now always a choice you make. Because the very moment you choose to surrender to Jesus, God sends the Holy Spirit to fill your soul. *For real*—remember God is supernatural?—the Spirit lives inside of you and fuels you with wisdom and power to fight your sin nature. The sin doesn't magically go away; you'll struggle with it until the day you go to heaven. But with Jesus, you have the God of the universe on your side to help you choose the right thing.

So I might go through the motions, but inside I'll be grumbling all the while.

That is not selflessness. That's as selfish as selfish gets.

Because when it comes to blessing others, what we do doesn't matter as much as our attitude toward doing it.

For the Lord searches every heart and understands every desire and every thought.

1 Chronicles 28:9

Are you willing to adjust your attitude? To dig deep and discover where your flaws might be hindering your ability to love others well? It's not a pretty process, I'll admit, but it is a huge and necessary step toward freedom, generosity, and joy. So let's unearth those attitude problems and toss them to the curb. Amen? I'll be with you every step of the way.

──────── Let's Dig Deeper ────────

1. What does it mean to be a sinner? Do you acknowledge that you are one? Why or why not?

2. Have you blamed others for your "junk"? How does Psalm 51:5 challenge the blame game?

3. Read Ephesians 2:8–9 and Titus 3:5. According to these verses, is it possible to earn a place in heaven (salvation)? How do we get in? (See Romans 10:9; John 14:6; and Acts 4:12 for more insight.)

4. Have you prayed for Jesus to save you from your junk (sins)? Tell someone about it!

5. See Jeremiah 17:9. What is the problem with the human heart? Now read Psalm 51:10; Ezekiel 36:26; Acts 15:9;

Hebrews 10:22; and 1 Thessalonians 3:13. Who fixes the heart problem?

6. How do you define selfishness? How does it show up in your life and your relationships?

7. Why does our attitude matter more than our actions? (See Ephesians 2:8–9; Proverbs 16:2; Jeremiah 17:10; 1 Chronicles 28:9; Psalm 44:21; and 1 Samuel 16:7.)

8. Have you been harboring a selfish attitude toward a particular person or responsibility in your life? Pray for God to change your heart in this situation.

Love in Motion

One of my favorite verses in the Bible is Psalm 51:12, "Restore to me the joy of your salvation, and grant me a willing spirit, to sustain me." Spend some time in prayer this week asking God to give you a renewed zeal for following Him. If you've never made the decision to accept Jesus as your personal Lord and Savior, what are you waiting for? Revisit the prayer of salvation and ask God to take over your life. It's the most important decision you'll ever make.

—— Chapter 3 ——

The "Me" Weeds

My husband keeps a small vegetable garden. He plants just enough tomatoes and jalapeños to produce about fifty pints of homemade salsa every summer. Also, he grows enough crabgrass to fill fifty pints more.

Weeds. Ugh. Where do they come from?! We toil and pray for the veggies to bloom—and some years they don't—yet those weeds spring up without the tiniest bit of effort. They choke out our tomatoes. They ruin the entire garden.

We all have weeds in our Christian walk, too. They're especially damaging to the "others first" process. Let's explore six common pitfalls of the sin nature that tempt us to think and act selfishly. I call them the "me" weeds.

Self-Absorption

How big is your world? In other words, how focused are you on your own little space in the room versus the larger home, family, community, and culture surrounding you? Each of us individually needs to look beyond our daily agenda, our appetite, our comfort, our bank balance, our problems.

Other people exist. They're taking up space all around us. And God wants you and me to get involved.

> Rejoice with those who rejoice; mourn with those who mourn.
>
> Romans 12:15

Of course, not everyone is called to hop aboard every cause. We each have to discern where God is asking us to serve. For me, that might be a moms' group at church; for you, maybe it's an African missionary hospital. God uses every individual believer in unique places to serve His kingdom as a whole.

However, when our only cause is our own well-being, then we're blind to the needs around us, and we miss the chance to bless others—which is, ironically, one of the greatest boosts to our own welfare we'll ever find. Pastor Rick Warren put it this way:

> God promises that if we will concentrate on blessing others, he'll take care of our needs. There's almost nothing that God won't do for the person who really wants to help other people. In fact, God guarantees this blessing. Jesus said, "I tell you the truth . . . no one who has left home or wife or brothers or parents or children for the sake of the kingdom of God will fail to receive many times as much in this age and, in the age to come, eternal life" (Luke 18:29–30 NIV). When you care about helping other people, God assumes responsibility for your problems. And that's a real blessing, for he's much better at handling your difficulties than you are.[1]

What thoughts and worries dominate your mind on a daily basis? What moves you and makes you overjoyed, angry, or sad? How do you prefer to spend your time, your energy, and your money? The answers to these questions will reveal where you fall on the spectrum between self-absorbed and outward-focused.

Pride

When we neglect to pull the weed of self-absorption, it creeps into our relationships as pride. Even though we may see other people around us and recognize their needs, pride strives to be right rather than do right by others.

For example, take a peek into my household on an average dinner hour not too long ago.

"Hon, those noodles are done," my husband announced as he stood over the stove and nodded to a bubbling pot.

"*I'm* cooking supper," I snapped. "Let *me* decide when the noodles are done."

"Uh, I was just trying to help."

"No, you weren't. You were telling me what to do."

Yikes. What's going on here? If I had listened clearly to the words my husband was speaking—and only the words he was actually speaking—I'd realize he was simply offering a helpful observation. But often my pride butts in with what I call the Becky Translation. And it causes me to misinterpret many a friendly conversation.

To demonstrate, let's replay the scene with subtitles.

Husband: Those noodles are done.

Becky Translation: You don't know how to cook noodles, wifey.

Me: *I'm* cooking supper. Let *me* decide when the noodles are done.

Becky Translation: I have a college degree, too, buddy. You're not the only smart one in this family. Just because you're slinging a briefcase and I'm sporting this frumpy apron doesn't mean I'm incompetent. I can handle the noodles! Get out of my space!

Husband: I was just trying to help.

Becky Translation: You don't know how to cook noodles, wifey.

Me: No, you weren't. You were telling me what to do.

Becky Translation: You think I can't do anything right. You're always criticizing me. Just let me live in peace, man! I know how to cook the stupid noodles!

Well, now. Let's look at this from a reasonable woman's perspective. Could it be possible that my husband was only trying to spare me the misery of soggy pasta? I mean, he knows how much I love a good bowl of linguini. What if—*gasp!*—my husband's benign comment was actually intended to bless me?

And I squashed his blessing with my big fat pride.

Ouch.

Beware the twisted "self" translations, and humble yourself to receive the giver's blessing.

> All of you, clothe yourselves with humility toward one another, because, "God opposes the proud but shows favor to the humble."
>
> 1 Peter 5:5

Entitlement

Another characteristic of selfishness is entitlement, or the "I deserve" weed. It sprouts whenever our pride takes root, like this:

I deserve to be treated better.

I refuse to talk about this problem.

I have a right to know what's going on here!

Oh, really? It's true that as children of God we have great inherent worth. But we must be careful about demanding our "rights." Because, as we've already established, we're sinners. And do you know what the Bible says about that? "When you sin, the pay you get is death" (Romans 6:23 NIrv). So heaven forbid we actually get what we deserve.

As Christians—saved from our terrible fate by God's love and grace—we're called to follow Jesus as our example. And even Jesus, the Son of God, did not claim His "rights." He crucified them.

> Think of yourselves the way Christ Jesus thought of himself. He had equal status with God but didn't think so much of himself that he had to cling to the advantages of that status no matter what. Not at all. When

the time came, he set aside the privileges of deity and took on the status of a slave, became human! Having become human, he stayed human. It was an incredibly humbling process. He didn't claim special privileges. Instead, he lived a selfless, obedient life and then died a selfless, obedient death—and the worst kind of death at that—a crucifixion.

Philippians 2:5–8 The Message

Envy

It's awfully hard to bless someone you're jealous of. When you're wishing for somebody else's stuff—their lifestyle, their looks, their money or talents—it's easy to see that person as competition. Which means—admit it—you'd rather see them kicked down than built up.

The envy weed blossoms in ways we least expect.

"Mom, Cyrus and Anna are really good readers." My younger daughter told me this news one day after I picked her up from kindergarten. "They go to their own special reading class because they are so, so good at reading. And Mom, they're reading *Charlotte's Web*! Isn't that really good?"

"That's wonderful, sweetheart." My nerves bristled even as I smiled at my daughter. "I'm glad you're happy that your friends are good at reading."

"Yep."

"You know," I said, "different kids are good at different things. Cyrus and Anna are good at reading. But you are good at math and playing piano, and lots of other things."

"I know, Mom." She shrugged as if those facts were irrelevant. I mean, we were talking about Cyrus and Anna here. What did *her* skills have to do with this conversation?

And that's when I realized—my daughter's intentions were pure. She was genuinely happy for her friends. There was not a shred of envy present anywhere in her mind.

But there was in mine.

I mean, come on, *Charlotte's Web*? In kindergarten?

39

I'll confess my first thought was this: *Your big sister read* Charlotte's Web *in kindergarten. So there you have it. We're smart, too.*

And my second thought was this: *Is my five-year-old falling behind???*

Oh, please.

Do you see how quickly envy and comparison can sneak in and twist an intelligent woman's brain? Instead of encouraging my child's desire to celebrate her friends, I turned my focus inward. I attempted to protect our own status rather than applaud someone else's. And I missed out on sharing with my daughter a beautiful quality that is quite the opposite of envy.

Sympathetic joy.

When was the last time you were genuinely happy for someone who got something you wanted? I'm talking joy unblemished by jealousy or self-concern.

The trouble with envy is that it makes life so much more complicated. We start questioning ourselves, our abilities, and our gifts. We doubt God's goodness toward us, as if He doesn't know what's best for us, or worse, He does, and He's refusing to give it.

We know better than that.

For the Lord God is our sun and our shield. He gives us grace and glory. *The Lord will withhold no good thing* from those who do what is right.

Psalm 84:11 NLT, emphasis added

So maybe it really is as simple as this: be happy for other people — period. Realize that another person's gain is not your loss. God ordains joy and sadness in every life. Let's support one another through it.

Distractions

On an hourly basis I probably check my phone a dozen times or more. Email, texts, weather, photos, Facebook, Instagram, Voxer,

Lord help me!—these are the weeds that vie for my attention at the same time my children are flipping cartwheels in the grass.

Don't get me wrong—technology itself is not the devil. I firmly believe Christians have a responsibility to use it for good. But as a work-from-home mom, it's dangerously easy to let work time leak into family time. And then I start looking at my loved ones as the distraction, rather than the other way around.

You too?

Fact is, it's impossible to bless someone you're ignoring. When we get distracted by external demands, we lose sight of opportunities all around us. Mobile devices aren't the only culprits. Distractions come in the form of stress, deadlines, overscheduled calendars, worries, fears, and so much more. Together these can breed a groundcover that hinders healthy shoots of perspective from poking through.

Until God slaps a hoe in the soil and tears those weeds out all at once. It looks kind of like this.

I sat at the family dinner table on an ordinary Monday night, cutting a pork chop and listening to my five-year-old rattle off her favorite activities of the day—recess, snack time, blowing bubbles in the yard.

Just then I reached for a forkful of rice and heard it—a strangled, guttural sound coming from across the table. My head jerked up, and in an instant I realized.

My eight-year-old daughter was choking.

In a single motion, my husband leapt from his chair, lifted our daughter over his forearm, and slapped a hand to her back. Praise God, the obstruction dislodged from her throat, and she spit it onto the table. I wrapped my arms around her and didn't let go.

In moments like that, a mom realizes what she has. And what she could lose.

"Are you okay?" I held my daughter's face in both hands and searched straight into her eyes.

"Yes, Momma," she whispered and nodded.

"Well, I guess we're not having those pork chops again!" My husband attempted to lighten the mood. But I knew it freaked him out, too. Our daughter sat on my lap for the remainder of the meal, although neither of us was hungry anymore.

The choking incident itself lasted a matter of probably seven seconds, but in my panic mode, I experienced the whole ordeal in slow motion. Then the adrenaline rushed throughout my body, and I fought back tears. Suddenly, I saw my daughter with fresh eyes.

Not as the girl I scolded two minutes earlier for poking her sister with a spoon.

Not as the child who would waste a perfectly good plate of vegetables, then ask for ice cream.

Not as the kid whose homework drains a portion of my dwindling energy night after night.

Again she was my gift. It was like the scales sloughed off my eyes, and for the rest of the evening and all the next day, whenever I looked at my daughter, I saw her more clearly for who she really is—a treasured possession on loan from God. And I shuddered to remember He has the right to take her away at any moment.

The question is—how am I spending the moments He gives me?

With my eyeballs glued to a screen? With my head swimming through to-do lists so that I'm physically present but mentally in a different galaxy?

It shouldn't take a life-or-death incident for us to realize how much our loved ones mean to us. Whatever busywork you had planned today, will you toss it aside for a minute and hug your children tight? Tell your husband you love him. Call a friend and laugh. Because none of our distractions truly matter compared to the people God gave us. Let's bless the people around us while we have the chance.

Above all, love each other deeply, because love covers over a multitude of sins.

1 Peter 4:8

Fatigue

Babies eat at midnight. Stomach flu strikes the house. Work brings on long days and sleepless nights. There are thousands of reasons to feel drained. And any woman who's ever tried to function on two hours of sleep knows that *tired* is just another word for *crabby*.

Sometimes we simply don't have enough energy to extend beyond ourselves.

I wish I had a perfect solution for that.

I don't.

But I do have a hug for you, my haggard sisters. I am one of you. In certain seasons of life, fatigue is unavoidable. So let's pray for God to grant us a supernatural degree of energy. Pray that He will keep watch over the door of our lips (Psalm 141:3), so we don't turn exhaustion into enmity.

And above all, sweet, sleepy friend, give yourself some grace. Not a single one of us is perfect, especially when we're tired. Focus on the blessings you gave well today, not the ones you withheld. Tomorrow is another day; a new phase is always around the corner—and life might look completely different after the Lord grants you rest.

> He gives strength to those who are tired. He gives power to those who are weak. Even young people become worn out and get tired. Even the best of them trip and fall. But those who trust in the Lord will receive new strength. They will fly as high as eagles. They will run and not get tired. They will walk and not grow weak.
>
> Isaiah 40:29–31 NIrV

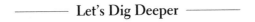

Let's Dig Deeper

1. Which of the six "me" weeds resonates with you most? Why?

2. In what ways does entitlement show up in your daily life and relationships?

3. Finish this sentence. *I deserve* _____. How does that statement compare to the truth of Scripture?

4. The opposite of pride is humility. What does it mean to be humble? How can a humble spirit enable us to bless others? (See Romans 12:3; John 3:30; Proverbs 11:2; Jeremiah 9:23–24.)

5. The Bible says love "bears all things, believes all things, hopes all things, endures all things" (1 Corinthians 13:7 NASB). In this context, to "believe all things" doesn't mean to be gullible or easily swayed, but rather, to love someone means you choose to see the best in them. Your view of that person is, by default, the best possible scenario. You desire to give them the benefit of the doubt. Is that true of your relationships? Why or why not?

6. Think of a situation in which you felt envious. What was your attitude toward the person you envied? How does envy make it difficult to bestow blessings?

7. Take a close look at your calendar. Does it reflect a focus on others? Or is the majority of your time and attention spent on self-concerns?

8. Have you ever been in a season of fatigue? Perhaps you're struggling through one right now. How does fatigue affect your relationships and hinder your ability to bless others? Are you praying to God for energy and grace? Be encouraged; He will give you the energy you need to pull through. "For the word of God is living and active and full of power [making it active, operative, *energizing*, and effective]" (Hebrews 4:12 AMP, emphasis added).

Love in Motion

Often we can be blind to our own shortcomings. On a scale of 1 to 10, assess whether you are more self-absorbed (1) or outward-focused (10). Then ask three close, trusted friends or family members to answer the same assessment about you. Do their answers reveal any blind spots?

— Chapter 4 —

The Blessing Toolbox

My older daughter learned to sew when she was seven years old. Over the past few years, she has accumulated quite a collection of sewing gear, from needles and pincushions and spools of thread to left-handed scissors, seam rippers, and her very own Singer sewing machine, a special Christmas gift from her nana.

Now when she wants to sew a pillow, my craftsy daughter can *sew that pillow thang*—because she possesses all the necessary supplies and know-how to get the job done.

Everybody needs a toolbox. No matter what kind of activity you're into—whether sewing or skiing or gardening or spelunking (whatever that is), it helps to have the right gear. And blessing people is no different. We need tools—meaning certain knowledge and strategies—to help us do it right. I call these the Blessing Toolbox. Let's examine eight core principles we must keep in mind when committing to bless other people.

Remain in the Vine

Have you ever tried driving on empty? It's impossible, right? With no gas in your tank, you can crank the ignition all you want, but that car is only going to choke and stall.

It's the same with God. We need Him like a car needs fuel, or else we're never going to get out of the garage.

I am the vine; you are the branches. If you remain in me and I in you, you will bear much fruit; apart from me you can do nothing.

John 15:5

In preparation for writing this book, I asked a few friends to accept an "outblessing challenge." Their job was to choose someone to bless consistently and intentionally for two months, then report back to me.

My friend Becky discovered an unexpected lesson.

My goal was to bless my husband and my children in how I talk to them—less direct, emotionless words and more kind, encouraging words. In all honesty, I failed the challenge. I struggled to purposely, consciously change my words to my family. In fact, my spiritual walk struggled for many of the weeks I was supposed to be doing this. However, I discovered something important about blessing others in the midst of this failure.

God showed me that when I was walking with Him, enjoying the presence of His company before anything else, not even thinking about purposely blessing others, I ended up blessing others! The time spent in His presence overflowed onto those around me without my having to consciously plan it. I gave generously to strangers on the street, I spoke kindly to those in my world, and it was all His doing. Him in me. When I wasn't walking with Him, when I allowed the demands of life to overtake time with Him, my focus was inward—and even consciously trying to bless others was difficult. I could do it, but something was missing. He was missing. The blessing became about my effort, and I wanted to be recognized for what I was doing.

The key to blessing others is this: Make God your top priority. Spend time with Him—praying, worshiping, reading your Bible. Deepen your relationship with Christ, and He will become so much a part of your character that His love spills over.

For it is God who works in you to will and to act according to his good purpose.

Philippians 2:13

This is what will distinguish you and me from the rest of the world, sisters. Anyone can do good deeds. But only Christians can bless with the unconditional love of Christ.

Start with Your Jerusalem

I don't like cooking. I mean, I do like food, but I just want it to show up magically, kind of like that lamb stew in *The Hunger Games*. That would be fabulous. There are so many other things I'd rather do besides cooking—and *need* to do, really, like writing, Bible study, plucking my eyebrows, whatever. I'm a busy woman. My to-do list never ends.

So when my husband pops his head through my office doorway and says something rude like, "Honey, what's for dinner?" I'm all like *Whaaaat?? Dinner?! Make yourself a sandwich, man. I'm on a deadline.*

The trouble is, my family needs to eat. And somebody needs to feed them. Yes, my husband can do the job (and often does), or we could order pizza (don't judge), but because I am a perfectly capable chef, I can't really justify not cooking for my people on occasion.

Here's a sticky truth. We are called to serve our families *before* we serve everyone else. In the first scene of the book of Acts, a risen Jesus appears to the disciples and commands them to spread His gospel story. He tells them, "You will be my witnesses in Jerusalem, and in all Judea and Samaria, and to the ends of the earth" (Acts 1:8). The ensuing chapters then describe the progression of Christianity from Jerusalem—the disciples' home base—out to the surrounding regions and beyond.

What does this mean for us? Essentially, ministry begins at home.

That's not to say we can't also serve others, spread our blessings around, and minister to the people next door or across the ocean—we'll talk plenty about that in the pages to come—but if we are blessing others and not our central family, or worse, blessing others consistently at the expense of our central family, then we've got the system all backward.

> If anyone does not know how to manage his own family, how can he take care of God's church?
>
> 1 Timothy 3:5

My friend and fellow author Courtney DeFeo knows this first-hand. As the founder of Light 'Em Up, a ministry encouraging random acts of kindness, Courtney spent a lot of time blessing her community. She told me, "It was fun and games for a couple months until I realized a very harsh truth—I was more excited and more motivated and more dedicated to being kind to absolute strangers than to my own family. Ouch." So she quickly readjusted.

"For an entire month, I focused on blessing my children first. I spent the same amount of creative energy sneaking around our house, finding ways to show I really did care about them—from little notes to treats and the like. It got my heart back on track. Now I believe I will never love others well unless I learn to love them first."

No Blessing Is Too Small

Diamond earrings are exciting. Tropical vacations are memorable. But a culmination of simple blessings can mean far more over time.

"When our son was new and I was adapting to first-time momhood," my friend Gina told me, "taking care of personal hygiene pretty much meant just a quick shower here and there, and it was kind of getting me down. In the 'olden days,' I used to love to take leisurely bubble baths and always had nicely polished nails. I will always remember the day my husband said, 'Honey, I'm going to take the baby for a while. You go soak in the tub and polish your nails.' I still get teary-eyed over that one."

Loving forward is a daily effort, a default; it has to be sustainable. Grand gestures are lovely, but they're not feasible every day. So don't assume you need to go big in order to bless another soul. No blessing is too small. Little things add up. And eventually, they infuse our ordinary routines with the holy fragrance of sacrificial love.

> Live a life filled with love, following the example of Christ. He loved us and offered himself as a sacrifice for us, a pleasing aroma to God.
>
> Ephesians 5:2 NLT

Be a Cheerleader

My older sister was a wrestling cheerleader in high school. Her squad sat on pillows beside the wrestling mat, clapping their hands and slapping the floor and chanting wild rhymes. Whenever a wrestler got stuck, straining every vein in his body against an impending loss, the cheerleaders cheered louder. They clapped harder. They wielded their mighty voices to pump up that young athlete until he found his strength again. Sometimes—believe it—their cheering actually made the difference between winning and defeat.

Words have a way of doing that.

How are you using yours?

I'll tell you one thing that can destroy a blessing even before it begins: criticism. And I'm not talking about the constructive kind. I mean insults, slander, or judgment. Or even saying nothing at all when what a person really needs is encouragement.

> The right word spoken at the right time is as beautiful as gold apples in a silver bowl.
>
> Proverbs 25:11 ICB

We have the power to affect people with our words. Ephesians 4:29 says, "Do not let any unwholesome talk come out of your mouths, but only what is helpful for building others up according to their needs, that it may benefit those who listen." Do you want to bless people? Speak kindly. Offer validation. Share truth with gentleness and respect. Cheer them on. If we're going to love generously, encouragement needs to become habit. That alone can shift the landscape around us.

> Gracious words are a honeycomb, sweet to the soul and healing to the bones.
>
> Proverbs 16:24

Play the Right Tapes

I've discovered a remedy for all my husband's annoying habits.

I stop thinking about them.

Like when he yanks open the microwave door two seconds before the timer beeps. Then later when I glance at the clock expecting to see something reasonable like 7:48, it flashes :02! :02! :02! —which tells me nothing except that there's a man in the house who wants to vex me.

Or when he walks three paces ahead of me in the grocery store, as if we're not involved in reading cereal labels and price-matching peanut butter together. Then once my arms are piled with jars and boxes, Mr. Speed Shopper is already in the next aisle —with the cart.

This stuff drives me nuts. I could spend all day stewing over it. But I don't.

Instead, I try to focus on all the stuff he does well.

My husband is loyal.

He is honest.

He's a hero to our kids.

He makes me laugh.

He knows how to replace a headlight.

I call this "playing the right tapes." For those of you under thirty, *tapes* in this case have nothing to do with the Scotch or duct variety. Once upon a time, tapes were those little plastic things we used to shove into the dashboard to play music, before cars came equipped with Bluetooth. You know, when George Washington was president.

On long road trips back and forth to college, I'd stick a mixed tape in the player, hit Repeat, and listen to my favorite tunes again and again and again until I could belt every word by heart.

That's how to love people. Memorize their positive qualities. And give them the benefit of the doubt.

> Whatever is true, whatever is noble, whatever is right, whatever is pure, whatever is lovely, whatever is admirable—if anything is excellent or praiseworthy—think about such things.

> Philippians 4:8

Forgive Quickly

When somebody hurts you, what do you do? Maybe you crawl into bed with a box of tissues, where you harden your heart and withdraw, resolving never to let anyone near you again. Or maybe you blow fire out of your nose and strike back, throw a hairbrush across the room (my personal vice), punch a few pillows, and cry out to God, "*Why, Lord, why me?*" Those are all natural reflexes. But consider for a moment one response that does not come naturally: forgiveness.

> Bear with each other and forgive one another if any of you has a grievance against someone. Forgive as the Lord forgave you.

> Colossians 3:13

Valerie is a women's ministry mentor, mom to three grown children, and a doting grandma. Among the ladies in her church, she is well-loved and admired for her wisdom and commitment to family values. Yet Val's relationship with her own mother has been strained since she was a child. The two women carry a history of tension, rooted primarily in her mom's relentless impulse to brandish her tongue like a knife.

This pain was more bearable when mother and daughter lived half a country apart. But when ailing health forced Val's mom to relocate nearby, Val had to learn to forgive, time and again, *in the moment*—for everyone's sake.

"When I start feeling those emotions of hurt and anger brewing inside of me, I realize I can't go there. I don't want to feed the beast," Val said. "Instead of letting my emotions control me, I need to let God's truth, His Word, control me. And the truth is that God is good, and this hopeless-seeming relationship is not, according to God's view, hopeless at all."

Val realizes a key truth of Scripture: forgiveness is a daily surrender—an ongoing choice to be hopeful, to love instead of hate, and to trust God and not ourselves. "In order to forgive my mom, I need to realize that she is broken, but so am I. In God's eyes, I'm no better than she is. Yet God has forgiven me. So I ought to do the same for her."

Does this newfound forgiveness mean Val's relationship with her mom is suddenly less hurtful or frustrating? Not at all.

"Don't get me wrong, my mom is just as annoying as ever," Val said. "But if I'm able to forgive her, I can enjoy her. I can laugh. I can have compassion. I can bless her. And my relationship with God grows stronger."

Show the Real You

I like to fill my Instagram account with pretty pictures of my children and me hugging and smiling, holding ice-cream cones, enjoying a harmonious family moment in which my forehead wrinkles have been photo edited and some witty list of hashtags beckons you to share in the joy of my awesome life.

But let's talk about what you don't see on Instagram.

Right now I am typing these words at a cluttered desk, overlooking stacks of *American Girl* magazines and craft supplies (because living the glamorous author life means sharing an office with a fourth-grader), and my right foot is sticking to the hardwood floor because my sock has a hole in it. My husband and I are currently in an argument over whose turn it is to empty the dishwasher, my fridge is filled with leftovers probably growing fuzz by now, and I'm half expecting a call any minute from the school office telling me my seven-year-old is barfing in the girls' bathroom because this morning I neglected to take her stomachache seriously.

That, folks, is real life.

And you may not find it on Instagram.

Actually, I should post that kind of stuff to Instagram.

Because you no doubt will relate to my honesty. And some desperate part of you will probably value it far more than my glossy pictures—lovely as they are.

Sometimes the best way to bless another person is to let them see the real you. Give them the gift of realizing somebody else's life is just as messy as theirs, and they are not alone. Not crazy. Not hopeless. Validate their concerns, let them know you've been there. Transparency prohibits walls from going up between you and me. It allows blessings to cross between us, unhindered. So embrace the raw truth, don't hide it. You might be surprised how well you can love another person simply by opening up.

Take Care of Yourself

Here is where I feel compelled to sit you down at my kitchen table, pour us each a cup of tea, and gently scold you for a bit, sister to sister. Don't worry—I won't dish out what I haven't already chewed on myself (for so long my jaw aches). But there's something I need to tell you; something you need to really hear and absorb into your bones. Can you take it? Hold my hand. We'll face this together.

You—my tired, beautiful friend—are you cranky? Drained? Stretched to the point of snapping and resentful of the people who demand your time, your attention, your blessings? *I've been there.* Some days I confess I live there still. It's time for us to learn to wield our final tool: self-care. By that, I mean thinking of yourself—yes, you!—even as you tend to others. It's a huge topic, wildly misunderstood, and it deserves its own book, for heaven's sake. But for now, this is what I want you to know. Let this truth anchor your every effort to demonstrate generous love.

Blessing does not equal martyrdom.

At first blush you might assume self-care and selflessness cannot coexist, as if one negates the other. But that is simply not true. Caring for ourselves is vital to the process. It's what refreshes us and enables us to do the work God gave us.

Take Elijah, for example.

In Old Testament days, Elijah was a prophet with great faith in God. He stood up to a powerful pagan queen and her fake god Baal—and won! Yet the queen, Jezebel, was so furious with Elijah for showing her up that she sent her men to hunt him down and kill him. Talk about a stressful ministry. So what did Elijah do?

He gave up. The poor guy actually ran away to the wilderness and told God, "I have had enough, Lord. . . . Take my life!" What?! Elijah, the super-prophet, wasn't just exhausted and discouraged. He was practically suicidal.

> Then he lay down under the bush and fell asleep. All at once an angel touched him and said, "Get up and eat." He looked around, and there by his head was some bread baked over hot coals, and a jar of water. He ate and drank and then lay down again. The angel of the Lord came back a second time and touched him and said, "Get up and eat, for the journey is too much for you." So he got up and ate and drank. Strengthened by that food, he traveled forty

days and forty nights until he reached Horeb, the mountain of God. There he went into a cave and spent the night.

1 Kings 19:5–9

Did the angel give Elijah a lecture? Did he give him a pep talk? Did he order him to pray or recite Scripture or go back home and do his crummy job? No. He fed him. Let him sleep. Gave him a chance to restore his strength, which restored his courage. As one of my pastors and others have said, "Sometimes the holiest thing you can do is take a nap."

God cares about your physical and mental well-being. He made you mortal, He knows your limitations, and He loves you. So take care of that body God created, the house in which His Spirit dwells. Only then can you fully realize your capacity to serve Him, and to love others well.

––––––––– **Let's Dig Deeper** –––––––––

1. Review the eight strategies outlined in our Blessing Toolbox. Which of these could you identify with most? Self-assess how well you handle each tool/principle (on a scale of 1 to 5, 1 being "I stink at this" and 5 being "I'm the poster child for awesomeness"). Highlight the areas you need to improve most.

	1	2	3	4	5
Remain in the vine	1	2	3	4	5
Start with your Jerusalem	1	2	3	4	5
No blessing is too small	1	2	3	4	5
Be a cheerleader	1	2	3	4	5
Play the right tapes	1	2	3	4	5
Forgive quickly	1	2	3	4	5
Show the real you	1	2	3	4	5
Take care of yourself	1	2	3	4	5

2. Consider your daily words and actions. Are you kinder to others (strangers, friends, co-workers) than you are to your family? Why or why not?

3. Do you have a tendency to dwell on negative thoughts or complaints about certain people in your life? Read 2 Corinthians 10:5. How can you apply this verse to your relationships?

4. Read Colossians 3:13–14. Discuss the connection between love and forgiveness in this verse. Why should we forgive others? How is our ability to love generously affected by our willingness to forgive?

5. Do you consider vulnerability a weakness or a strength? Read 2 Corinthians 12:9. How can getting real with others be a blessing to them?

6. Deuteronomy 4:9 (HCSB) says, "Only be on your guard and diligently watch yourselves, so that you don't forget the things your eyes have seen and so that they don't slip from your mind as long as you live." Consider how self-care is vital to keeping watch over your own soul. When you're burnt out, do you become kinder or crabbier? In other words, are you more or less likely to demonstrate the Christian virtues you've been taught?

7. To expand on the previous question—how can neglecting to take care of yourself diminish your witness for Christ? Conversely, how can self-care ultimately enhance your ability to bless other people and, in so doing, point them to God? See Matthew 5:16.

8. What additional "tools" would you add to the Blessing Toolbox?

Love in Motion

This week, choose someone close to you and shower them with small blessings each day. Practice the toolbox strategies to help you stay focused. What was the result?

— Chapter 5 —

Four P's of Blessing
#1 *Presence*

My brother-in-law and his wife live in Minnesota, near the Mall of America. I savor every chance we get to visit them because, well, I love them, but also because—IKEA. I mean come *on*, folks, thousands of square feet filled with trendy and functional household goods that a décor-challenged gal like me can actually use *and* afford. I get silly just thinking about it.

The showroom alone is well worth the five-hour drive. I wheel my blue shopping cart through the kitchen section—such pretty plates, spatulas for a dollar, a fruit cart—I *need* a fruit cart! Then the bathroom section—towels, soap dishes, shower hooks, oh my! And when I hit the home office section, well somebody slap me now because I could spend hours dreaming up my new desk space, my bookshelves, my pencil holders, oh my *goodness* have you seen the adorable little pencil holders?

Now, I can't say for sure, but I think heaven has an IKEA, and all the price tags are marked, "This one's on me—Love, God."

What's my point?

I want you to think of blessings like an IKEA store. Name it the Generous Love Supermart, filled with thousands of wares (blessings) in every size, shape, and color, all of which are organized into departments, or types of blessings. I call these departments the four P's: Presence, Possessions, Perspective, and Prayer. They are the main categories by which we can and ought to bless one another.

Over the next several chapters, we're going to explore these four P's one by one and discover the joy of giving through an array of applications. Got your shopping cart ready? Let's go.

Martha Gets a Bad Rap

I'm a work-from-home mom. Generally that means on any given weekday, I'm, um, home. Working. And September through May, during the hours of 8:30 a.m. to 3:00 p.m., life is good. Life is GREAT. My kiddos are at school, and I'm at my desk with my computer and my Google calendar—which is like the sun around which revolves our little planet Kopitzke.

But. Those outskirt hours? Those Saturdays and summer months? Wow, do I struggle. And I'm telling you right now, it's not my fault. It's my children. In fact, I'm convinced they're not actually children at all but sloths. I gave birth to sloths.

Sure, they pass for human beings, with their swishy ponytails and their full English sentences. But don't let them fool you. These girls morph into slow-motion mammals as soon as you tell them to move.

"Get your shoes on, girls. We leave for karate in five minutes." I rushed through the house, packing snacks and water bottles, smacking on a quick layer of lip gloss and searching for my phone.

Five minutes later, my children had not yet unglued their bottoms from the sofa.

"Girls! What did I say? It's time to go to karate. Turn off the TV and put your shoes on."

"I don't want to go to karate today," groaned the second-born creature. "I want to stay home."

"Too bad. You love karate. We're going. Put your shoes on."

"Do we haaaaaave to go?" Big sister sprawled her legs across the sofa. I clenched my fists, closed my eyes, blew steam out my nostrils, and counted to five—for me, not for them.

"Girls, what is our family rule?"

"Obeyyyyy the firrrrrrst tiiiiiiiiime." If sloths could speak, I'm sure they could not drawl those words any slower. My children know this rule. Yet the space between *knowing* and *doing* is where I live and train and discipline—and sometimes drive myself straight up the wall, which wouldn't be so bad if I had the sloth gene, too, and could hang upside down on the ceiling fan for a nice long nap.

How do I get through to these ~~marsupials~~ children?!

Mom is on a schedule! *Get in the van or get run over, people!!!!!!!!*

Hmmm.

Let's replay the morning at sloth speed.

While I was watching the clock, trying to squeeze in one more chore or email before the last possible minute to get into the shower or else run late (again), my girls were seated at the kitchen table drawing flowers and dinosaurs. "Mommy, look at my picture!" *"In a minute,"* I said. *"Mom is busy."*

When they ate their pancakes and asked for more, I answered five texts, switched two loads of laundry, and completely spaced the update that my kids were still hungry. "Mom, my pancake? You said I could have another one." *Oops.*

And while I barked at them to brush their teeth and comb their hair, I stood half naked in the mirror still fixing my own hair and makeup, clearly not demonstrating punctuality by example. Perhaps I could've gotten ready ten minutes earlier so I'd have time to cherish their pretty reflections and tell them how beautiful God made them.

Do you see the problem here? I expect my children to enter my world—my fast-paced, clock-ticking, hamster-wheel existence.

But I seldom bother to slow into theirs, to delight in their artwork or their silly songs, to answer their curiosity with more than half a brain of distracted attention in those moments when I have places to go and things to do.

And I suspect I'm not alone.

Do you do it, too?

This is not an issue exclusive to mothers. We can breeze past our spouses, friends, co-workers, neighbors, the lady on the sidewalk, or the gas station clerk. Every single one of us is shamefully prone to ignoring other people.

My daughters' dawdling might be a matter of disobedience, yes. But maybe it's also a digging in of sorts—a show of resistance against their mother's crazy pace. And if that's the case? I could learn a few things from my kids. Perhaps in the space between *knowing* and *doing*, I am just as disobedient as they are.

As Jesus and his disciples were on their way, he came to a village where a woman named Martha opened her home to him. She had a sister called Mary, who sat at the Lord's feet listening to what he said. But Martha was distracted by all the preparations that had to be made. She came to him and asked, "Lord, don't you care that my sister has left me to do the work by myself? Tell her to help me!"

"Martha, Martha," the Lord answered, "you are worried and upset about many things, but few things are needed—or indeed only one. Mary has chosen what is better, and it will not be taken away from her."

Luke 10:38–42

Does anybody else read that story and feel a prickle run through your nerves? I mean, have a little mercy here, Jesus. Let's go easy on poor Martha. Somebody has to feed the people, right?

However, when we really dig in to this passage, we see Martha's problem was not the preparations. We all have chores to complete, deadlines to meet, and mouths to feed. That's okay. God gives us work, and He wants us to do it well.

Martha's real problem was that she was *distracted*.

Look at your to-do list right now. Is your trouble the stuff you have to do, or your *attitude* toward doing it? Would you rather be somewhere else, doing something else, serving someone else — or perhaps serving no one at all?

Are you freaking out about everything that's expected of you and all the people demanding a piece of your energy? Is your to-do list causing you to get cranky with the souls around you — like Martha got cranky at Mary and Jesus?

Are you missing opportunities to bless people simply because you're too wrapped up in yourself?

If you realized you had a choice, tell me what you'd pick. Tasks and distractions? Or living in the moment, soaking up what matters, and offering your presence to the people who need it, who crave it, who — God says — *deserve* it.

> Do not withhold good from those to whom it is due, when it is in your power to act.
>
> Proverbs 3:27

Yes, I know those Martha tasks need to get done. But we must contain them within the bigger picture — because Jesus says those tasks are not the most important thing. Our *presence* is. *His* presence is. And how can we share it with others if we're too busy to look them in the eye?

What Does It Mean to Bless with Your Presence?

Throughout the Gospels, we see illustrations of Jesus modeling presence by stepping outside His agenda to grant time and attention to people around Him. He snuggles with children, heals broken bodies, and spells out spiritual lessons to His clueless disciples (poor guys, I can so relate). One fascinating example is described in the book of Matthew.

While he was saying this, a synagogue leader came and knelt before him and said, "My daughter has just died. But come and put your hand on her, and she will live." Jesus got up and went with him, and so did his disciples.

Just then a woman who had been subject to bleeding for twelve years came up behind him and touched the edge of his cloak. She said to herself, "If I only touch his cloak, I will be healed."

Jesus turned and saw her. "Take heart, daughter," he said, "your faith has healed you." And the woman was healed at that moment.

Matthew 9:18–22

Jesus was a busy guy. He had seriously important work to do. I mean, healing a dying girl? That's a pretty heavy itinerary.

Yet on His way to this urgent task, He stopped to acknowledge a woman who needed Him. He healed her; He blessed her. What does that say about Jesus? He is available, interruptible, and completely in tune to what's going on around Him, even in the midst of a demanding job.

So you want to be more like Jesus? Start there.

Blessing with our presence means giving our time, our attention, and our involvement. It means walking alongside another person—not setting pace from a distance or harping from behind. And it requires opening our eyes to really see the needs of others, then stepping beyond ourselves to serve those needs. This demands a willingness to take an interest in whatever interests the other person, whatever benefits the other person, whether it's our thing or not.

Do nothing out of selfish ambition or vain conceit. Rather, in humility value others above yourselves, not looking to your own interests but each of you to the interests of the others.

Philippians 2:3–4

As a mother, for example, do I really want to play checkers—again? Not usually. Maybe some of you do, and that's great. But checkers just isn't my top choice for recreation. I'd rather scrub the toilet, okay?

However, checkers is my child's favorite-favorite-favorite game in the family room cabinet. Therefore, investing ten minutes of my attention in sliding those little plastic discs across the board and letting her king me 'til she wins will bless my daughter in ways I cannot begin to measure. So I do it.

Or—do you truly enjoy raking a yard full of leaves and then trudging next door to rake for your elderly neighbor, too? Let's just be honest. You'd rather go inside for a nap. Yet this type of selfless offering—sacrificing your presence, your availability, your concern in the face of an everyday need—is exactly what our neighborhoods are starving for. And as Christians, we are equipped with the light of Christ to deliver authentic service and holy love just by being available.

The Farmer's Son

Carolyn is a farm wife near Waterloo, Iowa. Six years ago she was raising three kids, one in each age bracket—teen, elementary school, and toddler. She was busy and exhausted but loved her "normal" life, as she described it back then. She had no intentions of changing.

Until one day she drove into the city to visit her goddaughter, who was living in a run-down apartment with some other troubled youth. That's where she met Jasmine.

"There was this girl sitting on a dirty, bare mattress on the floor with this baby in a walker," she recalled. "He had beautiful blue eyes. It was cold in that apartment, and I remember he had bare feet. I could tell something wasn't right, that he was sick. My heart just ached."

Over the next several weeks, Carolyn couldn't shake the thought that the child needed help. She learned through her goddaughter that the boy, Aiden, was nine months old and suffering from a severe bronchial condition brought on by constant exposure to secondhand smoke. She asked to meet with Jasmine and, following what she and her husband believed was a nudge from God, offered to take Aiden for a week.

"We were not foster parents, we had no interest in adopting, nothing like that," Carolyn said. "But Jasmine put Aiden in my truck—me, a total stranger—along with all of his belongings, and she didn't see him again for months."

When Aiden arrived on the farm, he was in the tenth percentile for weight and had been fed only with bottles. Carolyn devoted her time to Aiden's grueling schedule of medicine and breathing treatments. "I did all I could to help him grow strong," she said.

Today, Aiden is a healthy six-year-old boy who loves to read and run and gobble up bowls of mac and cheese. Carolyn and her husband, John, officially adopted him and, later, his biological brother, Alex. The boys are growing up with older siblings who love them dearly, and together will one day inherit the farm.

As for Jasmine?

"She's like a daughter to me," Carolyn said. "When we legally adopted Aiden, I figuratively adopted her. She needed a mom. She so desperately needed love. When I was young I made similar bad choices, and she reminded me a lot of me. So I believe that if God can change my life, He can do it for her, too."

Taking an interest in other people can be risky. It might cost you time, effort, and heartache. It might even steer your life in a completely new direction, as Carolyn found out. But when we do it because *God says so*, we're never steered off course. On the contrary, He keeps us on His course. And He grows our hearts in the process.

Who's Got Time for That?

Blessing people with your presence doesn't need to be as dramatic as Carolyn's story. We've already established that no blessing is too small. The point is simply to identify a need, pray about how you can use your time or attention to meet that need, and then do it. Like Dana did.

"As a stay-at-home mom on a tight budget, I need to find creative ways of expressing my love language of gift-giving," she told me. "A friend was expecting her fourth child and mentioned she wished she could go on a date with her husband before the baby arrived. Her birthday had just passed, and her husband hadn't made plans to celebrate. I could tell she was feeling down, and I completely understood. I'd been wanting more 'date' time with my husband, too, but he had just started a new job and had very limited time for the two of us. So instead of complaining about my own situation, I decided to give my friend what I would want. I baby-sat her kids at my house and made it a play date for my kids, while she and her husband spent an afternoon out. Everybody had fun, it took my mind off my husband having to work longer hours, and I felt really good about the birthday gift I was able to give my friend that didn't cost me anything but time."

Ah. Let's talk about *time*. Quite frankly, I know some of you would rather toss dollar bills out the window than sacrifice precious minutes of your time. If I had more dollars than minutes, I'd lean that way, too. But that's the trouble, isn't it? Think about those words—*your time*. Is time really ours, after all? Or does our time belong to God?

> Many are the plans in a person's heart, but it is the Lord's purpose that prevails.
>
> Proverbs 19:21

The truth is, life on earth is short. Even if we live to a wrinkly old age, these mortal years compared to the breadth of eternity are "a mist that appears for a little while and then vanishes" (James 4:14). And when it does, God will ask us how we spent our mist. Why? Because He gave it to us in the first place. Every day, every hour is a gift from Him, the Creator of time and space. And He expects us to use it well.

> So be careful how you live. Don't live like fools, but like those who are wise. Make the most of every opportunity in these evil days. Don't act thoughtlessly, but understand what the Lord wants you to do.

Ephesians 5:15–17 NLT

Let's think of it this way. If my husband gave me an Apple Watch, would I let it sit in a drawer, untouched? No way. That thing is spendy, people. It's valuable. So of course I'd wear it. I'd use it. I'd thank him for it.

We should do the same with our time. It's more valuable than a million Apple Watches could ever be. So don't stash it. Don't hoard it. Don't toss it around carelessly. Use it to its maximum potential. Use it to spread generous love.

———— Let's Dig Deeper ————

1. Do you tend to get distracted by to-do's? What changes could you make to either your schedule or your attitude that would allow you to be better available for others?

2. Revisit the story of Mary and Martha in Luke 10:38–42. Do you relate better to Mary or Martha, and in what ways?

3. Why did Mary choose "what is better"? How can we make the same choice even when faced with tasks and responsibilities?

4. Encouragement is one of the most powerful forms of presence-based blessing. Read 1 Thessalonians 5:11 and Proverbs 14:1. Do your words and actions tend to build others up or tear them down?

5. Consider Carolyn's story. Has God ever called you to that degree of sacrificial blessing? How did you respond?

6. How do you feel about time? Are you a planner by nature, or do you go with the flow? How does your attitude toward time affect your ability to bless others?

7. Read Psalm 127:1–2. God says our work must be directed by Him, or it's of little use. How does this knowledge impact the way you view your schedule? How might it impact your prayers?

8. Read Psalm 90:12. What can we gain by asking God to help us make better use of our time? How can this help us love generously?

Love in Motion

This week, step into someone else's world. Choose an activity that your friend, spouse, or children enjoy (even if you don't), and spend time together engaging in that activity.

— Chapter 6 —

Blessings Near and Far

Hilary had a casual relationship with the couple across the street. She knew their names, knew they were both teachers, and every once in a while she'd walk over to say hi and pet their golden Lab, Bailey. But she hadn't spent much time getting to know them—until the day they brought home Bella, a four-month-old wiener dog.

"I love dogs," Hilary said. "I had just lost my own dog a couple months earlier, and I missed having a pet to take care of." She knew how much attention a puppy required, and that her neighbors were usually gone to work from six in the morning to four in the afternoon, so she offered to help.

"I was home during the day and figured it would be no trouble to let the dogs out at lunchtime," she said. And that's exactly what she did—every day for a year. She brought in the mail, let the dogs out and back in again, fed them a treat, and played fetch. If the puppy got into mischief, Hilary would clean up the mess and text the owners at work to alert them. Even once Bella grew old enough to forego daily breaks, Hilary continued visiting a few times a week just because it blessed *her* to bless her neighbors.

And the neighbors weren't just grateful; they were eager to bless her back. They gave gifts to Hilary's children, offered their snow blower in winter, and when Hilary's family adopted a new puppy of their own, the neighbors gladly dog-sat for a weekend.

Do you see? Blessing sparked more blessing. Not out of obligation, but in kindness and with genuine appreciation. And it all started because Hilary identified a need within her circle of influence and decided to meet it.

She offered her presence.

"The greatest reward," she said, "is not the reciprocating but the relationship we've gained. We consider each other part of our families now."

Presence vs. Present

Some of you might be wrinkling your noses at this point. *That's a nice story, Becky, but what if I don't have any neighbors across the street?*

What if I'm at work from dawn to dusk?

What if I'm on bedrest or contagious or deathly allergic to dogs and cats and dust and humans?

What if I'm living halfway across the world from the ones who really need me? The people I desperately want to bless?

Ah. Great questions. How can we give our presence when we can't actually be present?

It's simple, really. We need to upgrade our definition of *presence*.

Carry each other's burdens, and in this way you will fulfill the law of Christ.

Galatians 6:2

Being present does not necessarily mean being *in person*. With today's technology and infrastructure, we can be anywhere at any time—in voice, vision, or spirit. Our attentiveness actually travels quite well, if you think about it. Phone calls, note cards, Skype visits, texts. Snail mail! Glorious heaven, do you remember mail? Pens, stamps, Hallmark? These are the instruments of long-distance blessing. They enable us to "carry each other's burdens" even when we're apart. And in some cases, the act of loving generously may actually be more meaningful from a distance than it is in the flesh. Just ask these ladies.

My sister was having major neck surgery, and I was due to help her by preparing meals for the first two weeks of her recovery. But then I came down with a nasty cold and couldn't get close to her. She was at risk of infection and couldn't be exposed to my germs! I felt so helpless. So I sent emails to all my siblings and set up a food calendar with a rotating schedule for people to help her out. It was out of my comfort zone because it's easier for me to "just do it" instead of soliciting help. As it turned out, it was a big blessing for my siblings to share in our sister's care. —Vicky

While my husband was on active military duty in Iraq, he read bedtime stories to our kids via videos. We would send him the camera card in the mail once a week. It was his way of helping with bedtime even though he was serving our country. —Lisa

My ninety-year-old grandma lives a few states apart from me. With the time zone difference and the chaos of my family life, it is hard to call her on a regular basis. So I made a resolution to send her a card each month. I write—yes, with my hand—to tell her what's been happening in my life, and I also include a collage of photos I've taken of my three boys. It may be old-fashioned, but it makes me happy that she gets the connection to her great-grandkids even though we don't see her face-to-face or talk much. —Danielle

My little sister is fifteen years younger than me. When she was in college, I was busy raising three kids in a hectic household two hours away from her school. She was freaking out over finals one semester, and I remembered what it was like to need snacks and meals, so I called the Chinese delivery place near her campus and had her favorite dinner delivered with tip included. The next night I called in pizzas for her and her roommates. And later that week I had a huge arrangement of fresh fruit delivered for some healthy brain food, too. When you can't be right there to make a good home-cooked meal, delivery is always a good second option—especially for college students! My sister actually cried when the food was delivered.—Karyn

My husband makes a fresh pot of tea for me every morning before he leaves for work. By the time I wake up, he's usually already gone. But I can walk downstairs to the kitchen and find my hot tea, sometimes with a sweet note from him sitting next to the teapot. We've been married almost thirty years, and I'm celebrating nearly thirty years of tea.—Debbie

These people gave their time. They gave their encouragement. They gave their creativity and their communication and their solutions. They gave what they could, in the manner they could. And although they were not physically present, their presence was deeply felt.

It was a blessing.

About That Thing Ringing in Your Pocket

When I was a freshman in college, I lived in a tiny dorm room three hundred miles from home. My mom and I had a standing telephone date every Saturday morning at ten. This was in the Jurassic period, prior to unlimited talk and text plans, when phone companies had the audacity to charge thirty-five cents a minute for long-distance conversations.

Mom and I budgeted an hour a week. Those calls were a salve for my homesickness. I treasured them.

Of course, today's college students can update their mommas on Snapchat every thirty seconds if they want to. If only I'd had

FaceTime in my college days, maybe then my mother could've talked me out of that spiral perm my sophomore year.

Technology is a beautiful thing when we're separated from the people we love. But when we're in the same room together, quite the opposite is true. Technology can become the very thing that *separates us.*

How many times have you been to a restaurant and witnessed a family seated around a table, each of them thumbing their own mobile device and paying no attention to one another?

How many of you *are* that family?

Have you ever been in the middle of a conversation with someone when their pocket started ringing, and they pulled out their phone and answered it, midsentence?

Or how often have you heard about a dear friend's engagement, her pregnancy, or a death in her family through Facebook and not directly from her lips? Or at least in a private message, for heaven's sake.

It's an epidemic. We've become absent from one another's presence—even when we're face-to-face.

My mentor Judy and I make a point of scheduling quarterly coffee dates. As the women's ministry director of our large evangelical church, Judy is an extremely busy woman. She stays current on the latest high-tech communication, and she can speed-text with the best. Yet she still values old-school visits with the people in her life. I'm blessed to be one of them.

"With today's technology, distractions, and busyness, presence is even more of a gift," she told me. "A real, live person is more of a hot commodity than in the past."

Think about that. One hundred years ago, there was no television, no iPhones, no apps. People sat on porches and talked to each other. They wrote letters in full sentences, in which they actually expressed their feelings in words because emojis hadn't been invented yet. Can you imagine? How did anybody know when their friends were happy or sad or laughing till they cried?

Oh. They saw it in person.

They heard it in real life.

They experienced one another on an authentic plane of physical existence.

Don't get me wrong. We've already established that technology is not bad in itself, especially when you're miles apart. Technology is good! It's great! Go send your college student a text right now letting him know you love him!

And yet, if we're not careful, technology can and does create distractions that dilute our presence and steal opportunities to bless others. And that's a problem—because it belies the very nature of our identity.

"In every generation, since Adam and Eve, people were created to be relational beings," Judy said. "God himself is the Trinity: Father, Spirit, Son. He is in relationship with himself. And we reflect Him. We were created that way. We need to honor God with our interactions."

So call a friend today. Let her hear your voice. Schedule a lunch date with someone you love, go for a walk together, meet at the playground with your strollers and snacks, whatever works. I know we can't necessarily do this every day with every*one*. But from time to time, face-to-face connection with the people God gave us is still valuable. It's still relevant. It's still and always will be God's design for us as humans.

> And let us not neglect our meeting together, as some people do, but encourage one another, especially now that the day of his return is drawing near.
>
> Hebrews 10:25 NLT

That Girl Is Poison

Finally, I need to say a word to my fellow cranky women. You know who you are. I love you girls. I understand you. It's hard being us.

We get so pinched by *all the things*, right? Kids whining, husbands stressing, bosses bossing. It's just so easy to blow.

But you know what happens then. Physically we might be present, yes. But emotionally our presence produces a gas so noxious it chokes all the joy out of the room. We snap. We nag. We tell the kids they will never eat another potato chip again *as-long-as-I-live-do-you-hear-me?!*

I know I'm not the only one.

"Frankly, I have not been the easiest person to be around in recent months," my friend Tynea told me. "My mood is contingent on so many things, and a lot of the time my husband has been greeted with the cranky wife who has been worn out on mothering two young children. That's not fair to him, so I've been trying to bless him in the area of my attitude. It might not be my choice to have certain frustrations come up, but it is my choice how I respond to them."

Over the course of a couple months, Tynea made deliberate efforts to soften her tone of voice. She caught her tongue when criticism threatened to fly, and she spoke encouraging words instead. She remembered to smile when her husband walked in the door. She laughed at his jokes. And then one evening, out of the blue, her husband said, "You are so much fun to be around."

Tynea had not heard that comment in a very long time.

"I realized then that blessing someone doesn't have to be about doing something for them," she said. "Acts of service are great, and they can be very appreciated, but there's something about a person's attitude and demeanor that can be even more of a blessing. After all, who wants to be around someone who is grouchy all the time? May my attitude be one that breathes life into my relationships."

Ah. That's my hope for us all.

Now your attitudes and thoughts must all be constantly changing for the better. Yes, you must be a new and different person, holy and good. Clothe yourself with this new nature.

Ephesians 4:23–24 TLB

50 Ways to Bless with Your Presence

1. Look people in the eye when you talk to them.
2. Engage in meaningful conversations. Ask questions. Listen more than you talk.
3. Bring a friend a meal.
4. Send greeting cards.
5. Write your spouse a list of things you admire about him.
6. Offer to clean a friend's house.
7. Mow a neighbor's lawn.
8. Hug your children—and don't let go before they do.
9. Introduce yourself to the new woman at Bible study. Offer to sit with her.
10. Compliment someone.
11. Call your dad to talk about golf or fishing or whatever he's into.
12. Take your mother out to lunch.
13. Say "good morning" with a smile to everyone who crosses your path.
14. Give up your seat on a crowded bus or commuter train.
15. Carpool.
16. Mentor a student or young professional.
17. Read to an elderly friend. Invite her over for dinner and conversation.
18. Volunteer at church, your children's school, or a local community agency.
19. Sit beside your child and offer undivided attention when helping with homework or talking about his day.
20. Play a game with your kids.
21. Give your husband a back rub.
22. Let someone confide in you—and keep their confidence.

23. Organize a neighborhood Bible study.

24. Share the gospel with someone who needs hope.

25. Baby-sit for a friend's children with no expectation of payback.

26. Run errands for a friend who is ill or bedridden.

27. Shovel the neighbor's driveway.

28. Tell another woman she looks beautiful — on a day when she's wearing sweats or no makeup.

29. Ask "How are you?" then wait for the answer.

30. Do a chore that your spouse is usually responsible for (like taking out the garbage).

31. Write a note of encouragement for your child's teacher.

32. Smile at the person serving you in a restaurant, bank, store, etc. — and greet them by name. (They usually have name tags!)

33. Leave a note for your spouse or kids to read each morning before work or school.

34. Draw a smiley face on your child's sandwich baggie.

35. Text a Bible verse to a friend you haven't seen in a while.

36. Plan a Skype visit with your siblings.

37. Offer to drive your child's friends to church or AWANA.

38. Text encouraging notes to your husband while he's at work.

39. Share a special notebook with your child in which you write honest messages back and forth.

40. Exercise with a friend. You can hold each other accountable and cheer one another on.

41. Post love notes on your kids' bedroom doors.

42. Chaperone a field trip.

43. Be a safe place for friends to cry. Hand them tissues.

44. Hold the door open for others. Chivalry might be dead, but blessing is not.

45. Say "thank you" to people whose job is to serve you.

46. Kiss your husband and children good-night.

47. Schedule one-on-one dates with each of your children.

48. If you travel overnight, give young children an article of your clothing to snuggle with at bedtime. When they can't be with Mommy, a shirt that smells like her is the next best thing.

49. Reserve at least one night a week for focused family time. In our house, Fridays are pizza/game night.

50. When your child needs your attention but you're engaged in a conversation with someone else, teach her to lay a hand on your arm. Place your hand over hers to acknowledge her request. Then finish your discussion before tending to your child. This prevents interruptions and allows you to bless the person you're talking to with your undivided attention. It also shows our kids, by example, how we can be present for them and others at the same time.

───── Let's Dig Deeper ─────

1. Take a moment to consider your circle of influence. In your home, your neighborhood, your workplace, your child's school, your church—whom might God be calling you to bless in person? What needs can you identify and take steps to meet?

2. What prevents you from blessing others with your presence? What obstacles do you face?

3. Review Galatians 6:2. What does it mean to "carry each other's burdens"? What might this look like in your own life?

4. Discuss the pros and cons of mobile communication devices. How can we harness the power of technology for good purposes without allowing it to hinder our personal interaction with others?

5. Our God exists in three persons: Father, Son, and Holy Spirit. From the very first chapter of the Bible, God refers to himself as "us" (Genesis 1:26). Relationship is an inherent part of His character. Since we — men and women — are created in God's image (Genesis 1:27), we are also designed to be in relationship with one another. How does sin make this challenging? (Hint: recall the "me" weeds from chapter 3.)

6. Does your mood tend to taint your presence? When are you most vulnerable to being cranky? Pray for God to help you improve your attitude so you can breathe life into your relationships.

7. Read 1 Corinthians 13:1–7. Replace the word "love/it" with your own name. Is this passage true of you? Why or why not?

8. Review Philippians 2:5–11. How does humility — a kind and selfless presence — enable us to bless others well? How did Jesus model this truth?

Love in Motion

Choose one or more of the "50 Ways to Bless with Your Presence" and make it a priority to follow through this week.

— Chapter 7 —

Four P's of Blessing
#2 *Possessions*

My daughters take piano lessons. For several years, our family "piano" was a weighted electronic keyboard—a college graduation gift from my parents. It was handy for writing songs and plunking out notes for vocal practice, but once my daughters took up my love of music and started developing serious piano skills, they needed a serious instrument to match.

There was only one problem. Pianos are expensive.

My husband and I shopped around for a used instrument, but other expenses kept trumping the purchase. Somebody needed braces, the car broke down, our furnace choked and had to be replaced. Each time, we'd console ourselves with the fact that our kids still had a keyboard; it wasn't perfect, but it was adequate—for now.

Then one day I got an email from Paul, a bass player on our church worship team. He had overheard me Sunday morning talking about needing an acoustic piano, and he just happened to be looking for someone to take his—for free. Others had graciously offered to sell us theirs, but Paul's was a no-cost offer. He and his wife were moving and had no need for the piano any longer, and he simply wanted it to go to a good home.

"The Lord really blessed us with a great house at a great price," he told us. "We're so grateful to God for His provision. So we just want to pay it forward and bless somebody else. If you want the piano, it's yours."

My girls have been learning Beethoven and Mozart on that piano for two years now. It has beautifully suited our needs—and it didn't cost us anything but the pain of moving it into our living room.

Next in our four P's of blessing is *possessions*. Our stuff. Our money, our food, our clothing—our pianos—everything. Jesus never promises us wealth or poverty. He's not really that concerned about the stuff itself. But He does make it clear that what we *do* with our stuff is a test of our spiritual maturity.

> I tell you, use worldly wealth to gain friends for yourselves, so that when it is gone, you will be welcomed into eternal dwellings. Whoever can be trusted with very little can also be trusted with much, and whoever is dishonest with very little will also be dishonest with much. So if you have not been trustworthy in handling worldly wealth, who will trust you with true riches?
>
> Luke 16:9–11

What Does It Mean to Bless with Our Possessions?

The Bible is filled with directives to give, share, and tithe. Most of us would agree generosity is an admirable and prescribed trait of the Christian life. God owns everything, after all, and we're just the managers. "The earth is the Lord's, and everything in it. The world and all its people belong to him" (Psalm 24:1 NLT). Our job is to be wise stewards of what God has given us. He invites us to use our stuff to serve a purpose beyond ourselves.

Yet how many of us actually live that way day to day? Yes, you might give a percentage of your income to church or donate to world missions. Maybe you even make a habit of giving money to local charities or community ministries. Those are excellent practices, and "God loves a cheerful giver" (2 Corinthians 9:7).

But giving goes beyond tithing. This may sound harsh, so please understand my heart. Whether you're rich or poor, writing a check is easy. Getting up close and personal, however, and staring a human need in the face—ugh. That kind of giving can be hard.

Dare to Be Generous

"I was dropping off books at the library early one morning when I saw a homeless man was huddled by the door at the top of the steps," my friend Alicia told me. "I knew it would be several hours before the library opened and the man could slip inside to warm up."

Alicia was on her way to meet her husband for coffee, and she sensed God telling her, "Get this man a cup of coffee, too."

"Really, Lord? Are you sure? Because the downtown coffee shop serves the expensive kind of coffee." She thought about going to the gas station for a cheaper cup. But she immediately felt convicted.

"I heard the Lord speak to my heart. *Your husband is good enough for the expensive coffee, but this man is not? Remember, he is my child, too.* So I pulled back around to the library with a cup of fancy coffee and a scone. I realized that the Lord is lavish in His love for us, so I was going to be lavish, also."

> See what great love the Father has lavished on us, that we should be called children of God!
>
> 1 John 3:1

Alicia told the man her name and offered him breakfast. He introduced himself and started chatting. Alicia noticed he was listening to music, and when she asked him what it was, his response nearly knocked her over. "It was a *worship song*. He was sitting out there in the freezing cold, homeless and *worshiping*. I knew then that this man might've needed breakfast, but I needed a slap. Oh Lord, make my heart right."

Once again, generous love requires a shift in thinking. Just as blessing with our presence begs us to open our eyes to the needs around us, so does blessing with our possessions. And that's where many of us fall short. We don't want to see the need. We don't want to make the extra effort to meet it, or worse—we think we shouldn't or can't. But that's not what the Bible says.

> Teach those who are rich in this world not to be proud and not to trust in their money, which is so unreliable. Their trust should be in God, who richly gives us all we need for our enjoyment. Tell them to use their money to do good. They should be rich in good works and generous to those in need, always being ready to share with others.
>
> 1 Timothy 6:17–18 NLT

Just imagine. If all of us chose one person to bless with our possessions today, tomorrow, the next day—how might that change the world? God is constantly inviting us to get creative, to share what we have even when we think we don't have enough. This might require getting involved at a more personal level, like Alicia did. But never underestimate a divine opportunity to glorify God with our stuff and to make Him known.

> As a result of your ministry, they will give glory to God. For your generosity to them and to all believers will prove that you are obedient to the Good News of Christ.
>
> 2 Corinthians 9:13 NLT

Where Your Treasure Is

"Mine! Mine! Mine!" It's one of the first words a child learns to speak. Greed is an inbred characteristic of the sin nature, staking claims on "my" toys, "my" money, "my" car, "my" house. Americans in particular are entwined in a love affair with our possessions. We want them. We acquire them. We hoard them. (Remember my little IKEA fascination?)

Possessions are not bad. God blesses us with them; they can be part of life's enjoyment on earth. But they can't get us into heaven. And we can't take them with us once we get there. So loving our possessions more than we love God? Yep, that's bad.

> Do not store up for yourselves treasures on earth, where moths and vermin destroy, and where thieves break in and steal. But store up for yourselves treasures in heaven, where moths and vermin do not destroy, and where thieves do not break in and steal. For where your treasure is, there your heart will be also.
>
> Matthew 6:19–21

Of course no well-meaning Christian would say she loves her stuff more than she loves God. And yet what we do with our possessions ultimately reveals how we feel about the Lord. Do we trust Him to provide? Do we truly believe He owns it all? Do we seek our joy and our hope and our strength in Him more than in our material goods?

Are we willing to share our stuff? That's the big question. Because when we do, we're not just sharing our money or our meals. We're sharing God's love.

> Now, suppose a person has enough to live on and notices another believer in need. How can God's love be in that person if he doesn't bother to help the other believer? Dear children, we must show love through actions that are sincere, not through empty words.
>
> 1 John 3:17–18 GW

God Uses Our Blessings to Bless Us, Too

As a military wife, Tabitha and her husband moved around quite a bit. They'd been living on base in Tennessee for several months, and she hadn't yet met another wife she could confide in. So she prayed for God to bring her a friend.

Around this same time, Tabitha saw an ad for a baby products giveaway, and she entered the drawing. Although her child was no longer in diapers, she figured, "If I won the prize package, God would show me who to give it to."

And He surely did. Tabitha won the giveaway just days before her husband invited a new soldier and his wife to join them at church. When she learned the couple had a two-month-old baby, she knew God had answered both her prayers.

"I felt my heart wanting to help her," Tabitha said. "She was surprised that I would do something nice for her. She hadn't seen any kindness from the other military wives yet. She needed a friend just like I did."

The two women are now close confidantes. They support one another through the challenges of motherhood and military marriage, and they share the same faith in God, who brought them together.

"I love how God used something I meant for blessing someone else as a way of blessing me, as well," Tabitha said. "He sees ours needs, and He answers them."

Operation: Agent Rusty Fish

Has it ever occurred to you that *you* might be the answer to someone's prayer? God often works through us, His faithful children, to provide for other people's needs. Our part of the deal is to keep our eyes and ears open to the needs of those around us, and then to act when we sense God telling us, *Here's a chance to bless someone—do it.*

This kind of generous awareness has a name. It's called Agent Rusty Fish.

Mike is an elder on our church board. He and his wife, Vicky, have been married over thirty years; they raised a godly daughter,

Carli, who is now raising three boys of her own. My husband and I enjoy gleaning this wonderful couple's wisdom on parenting, marriage, work/life balance, and especially how to navigate the treacherous terrain of teenage girls.

They have a lot of stories to share. This one is my favorite.

When Carli started high school, Mike and Vicky wanted to instill in her an awareness of other people's needs. They knew teens are easily influenced by today's self-absorbed culture, so they devised an intentional plan for growing Carli's outward focus—through gift-giving.

Carli's job was to keep her ear to the ground and identify struggles among the kids at school, then share them with her parents. As a family, they prayed over these opportunities and decided how and when to help—anonymously. They named their covert operation "Agent Rusty Fish," after a silly rustic metal fish lantern hanging at their cabin.

For example, Carli learned that a boy at school wasn't getting enough to eat, so she and her parents bought restaurant gift cards and fashioned a note out of cut-up newspaper letters, signed "Agent Rusty Fish." Another student badly needed a car repair, so the family stuffed cash in an envelope along with an incognito message from Agent Rusty Fish. One young man, an avid skier, had broken some important ski equipment, so Agent Rusty Fish gave him a gift card to a ski shop.

The gifts were intended not only to provide financially but also to encourage the recipients emotionally and spiritually. "The notes that we included were always written to build up these kids," Vicky said. "Often we thought the notes, which were sometimes pretty long, were the best part of the gift!"

Delivering them was also part of the adventure. "Carli and I would hide in the car, out of sight, while Mike ran up to the door and rang the doorbell," Vicky explained. "We'd already have an escape route all planned out, so as soon as the deed was done, Mike would run back to the car as fast as he could while we caught a peek of the person opening their door to find nobody standing there—just a gift and a wacky note from Agent Rusty Fish. We had such a blast blessing people this way!"

Kids received funds for clothes, recreation, and any variety of needs. Soon students all over school were talking about their surprise gifts from Agent Rusty Fish. These teens wondered who in the world could have known to give them just what they needed when they needed it. Agent Rusty Fish became something of an urban legend, and until now (a decade since), nobody had a clue exactly who was behind the secret blessing operation.

(I love this story so much, I begged Vicky to let me blow her cover. Let's honor her generous confession by establishing an epidemic of Agent Rusty Fish in schools across America and all over the world—are you in?)

Perhaps the greatest reward for Vicky and Mike was seeing their daughter's character grow as she intentionally listened for other people's needs and invited her parents to respond. "It was such a blessing to cultivate a spirit of *giving*," Vicky said. "And it's still a big part of Carli's life today."

Make blessing a family affair. Listen for needs, pray about how God might want you to meet them, and do it—in secret, if you wish. Why? Because it's crazy fun. And God will bless you for it.

> Give your gifts in private, and your Father, who sees everything, will reward you.
>
> Matthew 6:4 NLT

———— Let's Dig Deeper ————

1. Review Psalm 24:1. Who owns everything? How should this truth affect how you manage your money and possessions?

2. Refer to 2 Corinthians 9:7. Are you a cheerful giver? Or do you have a hard time parting with your stuff? Why?

3. Read Mark 12:41–44. What does this passage teach us about sacrificial giving? Why is generosity so important to Jesus?

4. Read Matthew 6:1–4. What does this passage say about giving in order to get? Why would boasting about our generosity nullify the good deed?

5. Review Malachi 3:10. Do you trust God to bless your generosity? Why or why not?

6. Matthew 6:19–21 tells us to "store up . . . treasures in heaven." What have you been storing up? Earthly treasures, or eternal treasures? Discuss what this looks like in your life.

7. Think of a time when you were the recipient of possession blessings. How did it affect you?

8. Read the parable of the talents, Matthew 25:14–30. In this story, the master is God and the servants are us—God's people. Which servant can you identify with most? Why do you think the master was upset with the servant who made no effort to invest what he was given? What steps can you take today to invest wisely what God has given you?

Love in Motion

Start an "Agent Rusty Fish" operation in your family. If you have children or grandchildren, encourage them to listen for needs among their friends and classmates. Pray together about how you can meet those needs, then have fun blessing with your possessions!

— Chapter 8 —

Olivia's Heart

Olivia was a beautiful child in every way. A quiet, gentle spirit, she had a tender heart toward people and a smile that sparkled with kindness. The eldest of three, she was a nurturing big sister and her momma's shadow—shy, dependable, affectionate. She loved Bible stories and often spent daddy-daughter dates at the mall handing out gospel tracts. Her favorite color was blue, a fitting choice, the color of royal blood. Olivia knew without a doubt she was a beloved daughter of the King.

On a mild Sunday evening in May, when she was just eleven, Olivia was called home to Jesus in the same tragic shooting that took her father, Jon, and wounded her mom, Erin, whom you met in the first pages of this book. It's natural for us to say Olivia was taken too soon and to mourn the brevity of a life filled with so much promise. Yet for the Christian, grief is inseparable from hope. We believe God knows what we cannot comprehend; therefore, we trust Him even when it hurts. And we cling to the truth that one day Mother and Father and child will be reunited with their Savior for eternity.

"Olivia had a spiritual maturity beyond her years," Erin said. "She loved to talk about things of the Lord. She understood the gospel and she *desired* it. She wanted to know God."

Overflowing from her heart for Jesus was an inherent sense of compassion and generosity. "Olivia was a giver. She'd save up her money to buy presents for other people," Erin said, remembering how one year Olivia spent her own birthday money on a Valentine's Day gift for her parents. "She'd leave notes around the house for us. She was very caring, loving, thoughtful, and selfless. She put others before herself."

In honor of what would have been Olivia's thirteenth birthday, friends organized a community-wide campaign called Olivia's Heart. Participants were invited to perform random acts of kindness throughout the day to encourage strangers, loved ones, and anyone in between. A dedicated social media page described the purpose and hope for this effort:

"Pray for this event. That light would shine through the darkness. That God again would have victory and receive all the glory. Pray that Olivia and her story will reach those who aren't saved."

On the appointed day, hundreds—possibly thousands—of people answered the call. They delivered small gifts and gestures in a variety of forms, each time accompanied by a note attributing the generosity to Olivia and her heart for sharing Jesus.

People stuffed money orders in mailboxes. They gave gift cards to single moms and flowers to gas station clerks. They paid for strangers' groceries and tucked candy canes under windshield wipers.

Families delivered cookies to the fire department. Handed hot coffee to crossing guards.

They donated funds to charity. Distributed treat bags to hospital staff. Doubled the server's tip at lunch.

All throughout our area, Christians taped dollar bills to vending machines, plugged quarters into parking meters, placed chocolates on co-workers' desks. Countless acts of giving were gladly bestowed and recorded on social media.

And then?

Oh, it was such a thing to behold.

The recipients started spreading generous love.

Soon people who hadn't even heard about Olivia's Heart—until the moment someone paid for their meal or handed them a gift—were inspired to propel the blessing. Moms brought hand warmers to teachers on recess duty. Co-workers bought bagels for the break room. Police officers distributed stuffed animals to children—and so much more. All in honor of sweet Olivia and for the glory of the God she loves.

Olivia's Heart generated an amazing outpouring of story after story, courtesy over courtesy, blessing upon blessing as a community pulled together and strengthened in faith through giving—all because one little girl had a God-given desire to bless others, and those who remember her wanted her legacy to shine.

If You Give Our God a Fish

Olivia's Heart showed our community that sacrificial giving works. It opens hearts. It shifts moods. It changes people. Like this woman.

My daughter didn't like what her cafeteria was serving for hot lunch. So I rushed to McDonald's to surprise her at school with a Happy Meal. In the drive-thru, I got behind a white van that had a window sticker of seven little owls. Beneath it read the words, "Yes, these are owl our owls." And I thought, *Oh great, if this van has all these little owls with them, I am never going to get to school on time!* So during the fifteen-minute wait, I grew more and more impatient and made some unkind facial expressions into the van's rearview mirror. When I finally got to the window, the server delivered my food along with a five-dollar gift card from "the lady in front of me." Boy, did I feel like a jerk. So, to the family in the white van, I am so sorry for being rude behind you. After all, you were just trying to feed your kids like I was trying to feed mine. Thanks for reminding me to slow down.—A fellow mom

When we give someone a gift, we spark an invocation. Maybe to us it's just a card or a cup of coffee—small, even inconsequential offerings, we might say. But God doesn't see it that way. He has the power to use that gift. He can multiply it. He can make miracles with it.

Remember this story?

> Jesus soon saw a huge crowd of people coming to look for him. Turning to Philip, he asked, "Where can we buy bread to feed all these people?" He was testing Philip, for he already knew what he was going to do. Philip replied, "Even if we worked for months, we wouldn't have enough money to feed them!" Then Andrew, Simon Peter's brother, spoke up. "There's a young boy here with five barley loaves and two fish. But what good is that with this huge crowd?"
>
> "Tell everyone to sit down," Jesus said. So they all sat down on the grassy slopes. (The men alone numbered about 5,000.) Then Jesus took the loaves, gave thanks to God, and distributed them to the people. Afterward he did the same with the fish. And they all ate as much as they wanted. After everyone was full, Jesus told his disciples, "Now gather the leftovers, so that nothing is wasted." So they picked up the pieces and filled twelve baskets with scraps left by the people who had eaten from the five barley loaves.
>
> John 6:5–13 NLT

I read this Bible passage to my older daughter one evening when she was about five years old. "What's special about this story?" I asked her.

"Ummm . . . the boy gave Jesus his fish?"

"Yes, the boy was very kind to share his fish and bread with everyone." I nodded. "But what did Jesus do with it?"

"He made it grow bigger so everybody could eat."

"Yes! Isn't that amazing? The lunch basket wasn't magic. The boy wasn't magic. But Jesus has superpowers. *He* is the star of this story."

Ahhh. My daughter got the picture just as a light bulb went off in my own head.

Sometimes I'm like that little boy.

I think I have nothing much to offer. If only I were independently wealthy, right? Then I could give millions to world missions! I'd build shelters for the homeless and fund a cure for cancer! I'd donate Hawaiian vacations to every teacher and nurse and police officer in town! I'd splurge on the singing birthday cards, people — the eight-dollar cards, for the love!

Eh, but too bad. I'm frugal. My budget requires it. So that check to world missions might be missing a few zeros. Teacher appreciation gifts are more likely jugs of Hawaiian punch. And for your birthday, my dear friends, you'll get a Dollar Store greeting card and a phone call — or better yet, a coffee date — because I'll bless you with my presence. Of course.

Not much of a feast, perhaps.

But — so what? Maybe just the thing Jesus needs in order to feed the multitudes is my basket of wimpy fish. How easily I forget that God can transform a humble offering into something bigger, better, beyond imagination. The wow factor is His job, not mine.

Jesus didn't just feed people's bellies. He filled their souls. And let's not miss the fact that He didn't actually need that starter batch of fish and loaves in order to work a miracle. Jesus can create those out of thin air. Could it be He wants to use our ordinary gifts and steps of faith to launch great things?

Fish and Loaves, Blankets and Clothes

Jamie lived in a city in Maine that housed a large refugee population. These transplanted families inhabited the poorest area of the downtown district, intermingled with homeless people and street addicts. One of the pastors of Jamie's church was particularly drawn to serving these residents.

"I belonged to a small moms' group, and we wanted to do more than Bible studies," Jamie said. "We wanted to show our faith in action." So they joined forces with their pastor and held a blanket drive at the church.

The group asked its congregation to donate gently used blankets for refugees and others living in the darkest corner of their community. The request in itself was a challenge. "The culture in our town was not one of wealth or grand generosity," Jamie explained. "These were very hardworking, barely middle-class people. It was not uncommon for someone to work two or three jobs just to pay the bills. So people didn't part with their stuff easily."

And yet. Within a few weeks, the moms had collected more than a hundred blankets and a few sheet sets, which they took to a downtown food pantry and distributed to people in need. There they found families not entirely unlike their own—living day by day, trying to feed their kids and love one another through challenging circumstances. "We had such a tremendous desire to be relevant and to help," Jamie said. "But by getting to know these people, I think they blessed us just as much as we intended to bless them."

Encouraged by the blanket drive's success, the group decided next to collect clothing and school supplies for refugee children. Six months later, they were back at the food pantry with an abundance of items. "We continued to take donations, and within a year we had a supply of summer and winter clothing for kids and adults and had started handing them out two to four times a year," she said.

Best of all, the group's efforts enabled their pastor to build relationships with the people downtown, where he and the mom volunteers tended not just to people's physical needs but also to their souls. "One time, we were able to pray for a woman and help her get into rehab," Jamie said. "She decided right on the spot when she saw us that God had sent us."

What began as a blanket drive has now grown into a thriving daily ministry. Jamie's pastor opened a rehab facility next door to the food pantry, where the congregation continues to distribute donated clothes and supplies. Although Jamie has since moved to a new state, she still follows the group's progress and marvels at how God used a dozen women and one thrifty congregation to serve thousands of residents and counting.

"It was totally God in the lead," she said. "He was just lavishing His love on all of us."

That is what our God does. Are you willing to take a step of faith, to share your material goods and lift them up to the Lord? He can make much of little. And—*praise Him*—the world will start to notice.

50 Ways to Bless with Your Possessions

1. Pay for someone's groceries in the checkout lane.
2. Bring hot cocoa to a crossing guard.
3. Go to the Laundromat and pay for someone's wash.
4. Tape packages of microwave popcorn to Redbox machines.
5. Leave a tip equal to or greater than your restaurant bill.
6. Donate to a friend's adoption fund.
7. Host an in-home shopping party and donate the hostess rewards to a family in need.
8. Sell an item on Craigslist, then surprise the buyer at pick-up by giving it for free.
9. Give a gift card to the employee in the drive-thru window.
10. Visit a local elementary school office and ask staff to identify a child with financial need. Offer to pay that child's food voucher account in full.
11. Leave bags of groceries on a friend's doorstep.
12. Buy meals for homeless people.
13. Assemble a care package for someone in need of a smile.
14. Buy good quality seasonal clothing or household items on clearance (hats, mittens, etc.) and donate them as needs arise throughout the year.
15. Leave a cupcake on a co-worker's desk.

16. Give a gift card to a teacher.
17. Pass gift card balances to the customer behind you in line.
18. Identify a child a size or two smaller than yours and pass down outgrown clothing and shoes.
19. Tape coupons to popular grocery store items.
20. Pass around books you've read, especially to those who can't afford to buy them.
21. Donate to community agencies, such as giving nonperishable goods to a food pantry or hygiene products to a domestic abuse shelter.
22. Drop off gift baskets filled with goodies for a single mom and her children.
23. Rather than trading in your vehicle for a new one, donate it to a family who desperately needs a car.
24. Tape coins to vending machines or parking meters.
25. Pay someone's library fines.
26. Distribute gift cards or treat bags to people who serve you— such as your daycare staff, postal carrier, auto mechanic, store clerk, librarian, bank teller, dental hygienist, barista, etc.
27. Anonymously pay the restaurant bill for teachers, veterans, pastors, or elderly couples.
28. Send care packages to military service men/women or lonely college students.
29. Buy a monthly subscription service for a friend. Subscription gifts run the gamut from chocolate boxes to devotional kits to craft supplies, makeup products, fresh fruit, and so much more.
30. Pay for a youth group to attend a movie or concert.
31. Give money toward someone's mission trip expenses.
32. Donate shoes to Soles for Jesus (SolesForJesus.org).
33. Cover the cost of a child's summer camp registration.

34. Give a Bible to a stranger.
35. Sponsor a child through Compassion or a similar ministry.
36. Buy treats from the ice-cream truck for all the kids in the neighborhood.
37. Donate new books to the library.
38. Hide a dollar in a library book.
39. Leave new buckets and shovels at the playground sandbox.
40. Host a rummage sale or lemonade stand and donate the profits.
41. Donate devotional books to a doctor's office waiting room.
42. Contribute annually to Toys for Tots and Operation Christmas Child.
43. Send dessert to another family's restaurant table.
44. Pay for someone's highway toll.
45. Take a deployed service man/woman's family out for ice cream.
46. Ask birthday party guests to contribute donations rather than gifts.
47. Buy extra school supplies for a school on a tight budget.
48. Share a taxi and pay the entire fee.
49. Give a candy bar to a bus driver.
50. Keep dollar bills in your wallet to hand out to children "caught" doing good deeds.

——— **Let's Dig Deeper** ———

1. Why does it surprise us when someone—especially a stranger—behaves generously? What does that say about the state of our culture?

2. Consider this chapter's story of the woman in the McDonald's drive-thru. Could you relate to her impatience? She came to

her senses when the car in front of her gave her a gift card; however, how can a godly perspective help prevent the impatience in the first place?

3. Do you believe you don't have enough to give to others? What does God's Word say about that? Review John 6:5–13, and see 2 Corinthians 8:12.

4. What "ordinary gifts" can you offer to someone this week?

5. Has God ever nudged you to give in a manner that seemed impossible to you at the time? How did you respond? What was the result?

6. Jamie's story demonstrates how material blessings can pave the way for relational and spiritual blessings. Read Luke 6:37–38. How does this passage support the idea that a generous spirit is much more than economic?

7. Who among your sphere of influence is in need of possession blessings? What prevents you from taking action to help meet their needs?

8. Which of the "50 Ways to Bless with Your Possessions" interests you most? Which could you do today?

Love in Motion

Choose a closet or cupboard to declutter this week. Box up what you no longer need and donate it to a local charity, thrift shop, or a family in need.

— Chapter 9 —

Four P's of Blessing
#3 Perspective

My firstborn daughter is a little mother hen. Nurturing, methodical, bashful—she loves dolls and baking and singing and school. She's a lot like her mom.

So when my second daughter was born, I anticipated another mini-me. What we got was a loud, boisterous tomboy who prefers action figures over fairy wands. She is a source of constant entertainment, spunk—and bewilderment.

Of course I cherish both my girls. Yet in order to truly love them well, I need to recognize and embrace who God created them to be, regardless of how that jibes with my expectations.

We all need to do this, with all people.

But the Lord said to Samuel, "Don't judge by his appearance or height, for I have rejected him. The Lord doesn't see things the way you see them. People judge by outward appearance, but the Lord looks at the heart."

1 Samuel 16:7 NLT

In the Old Testament, God sent the prophet Samuel to a farmer named Jesse. His charge was to identify from among Jesse's sons the man who would become king of Israel. Jesse paraded seven strong and able young men before Samuel, yet each time the Lord told the prophet, no—he's not the one.

Finally the youngest son, the runt, a mere sheep herder, was the only choice left. Jesse reluctantly allowed the boy to show his face, at which point God said, yep, he's my man; I choose this kid to carry out my work on earth. Pick him.

David.

Ahhh. And who did this shepherd boy become? Only the greatest king in Israel's history, mighty warrior, author of psalms, a man after God's own heart. God saw all of this in David, before anyone else—even a prophet—could.

Guess what? God sees the potential in you and me, too.

> For we are God's handiwork, created in Christ Jesus to do good works, which God prepared in advance for us to do.
>
> Ephesians 2:10

Blame it on the sin nature—we're awfully quick to judge other people by their appearance, their behaviors, their background, their mistakes. We judge strangers. We judge friends. We judge the very people sitting around the family room with us, eating popcorn on Friday nights. We expect they ought to be *this* kind of person when indeed God has created them to be *that* kind of person—and He chooses them, values them, loves them just the same.

Shouldn't we, too?

Next in our four P's of blessing is *perspective*: how we see people, how we shed bias and misconceptions and keep our eyes open for opportunities to love and bless others—especially people who are different from us. In our churches, our communities, our workplaces and homes, perspective is a key ingredient in loving the way Jesus loves.

Accept one another, then, just as God accepted you, in order to bring praise to God.

Romans 15:7

Let's examine five aspects of a godly perspective that will empower us to love generously.

Perspective Check #1—People Belong to God

I boarded the plane, squished my carry-on bag inside the overhead compartment, and buckled into a window seat. I'd just finished an exhausting four-day conference halfway across the country and was eager to get home to my family. Napping through the flight was top of my to-do list; chatting was not.

Within a few minutes, a middle-age man with cropped hair and khakis settled into the seat beside me. At first I hoped we'd ignore each other; he closed his eyes through the oxygen mask demo, and I guessed he was either nervous or tired or both. Actually, he was just bored.

"You heading to or from?" He cracked one eyelid and turned his head slightly toward me.

"From." I smiled. "Wisconsin is home. You?"

"Well, I'm headed to Milwaukee for a few days. Just came from a seminar in Raleigh. Then I'm on to Detroit and Atlanta and a short stop in D.C. before I get a break. I travel a lot for work."

No kidding. Turned out my seatmate was a federal agent whose job involved training police officers all around the country on racial profiling and prejudice. His objective was to break through perception barriers so everyone in the nation is given a fair shake.

"Every time I get on a plane," he said, "I imagine it's my first flight. No bias based on my previous experience with airplanes, even though I've been on hundreds of them. I believe people should treat each other in that same way."

Wow. Suddenly I was glad I hadn't napped. My new fed friend taught me a lesson I should have known well from my Bible:

Approach each and every person as an individual worthy of respect.
No preconceived assessments based on their economic or social
status, what they're wearing, or how they talk. Just see them for
who they truly are—God's created one.

> Know that the Lord is God. It is he who made us, and we are his;
> we are his people, the sheep of his pasture.
>
> Psalm 100:3

Here's where I need to pause and make an important distinction.
Did you know? All people are God's creation. But only Christians
are God's children.

> But to all who believed him and accepted him, he gave the right
> to become children of God.
>
> John 1:12 NLT

Once we surrender to Jesus as our Lord and Savior, we are more
than God's possession, more than His masterpiece—we are His
heirs (Romans 8:17). How awesome is that?

Sadly, though, our role as God's children can create a superiority
complex in some Christians.

Don't let it.

Because although believers may be set apart, remember that
God loves the whole world (John 3:16), and He doesn't want
anyone to perish (2 Peter 3:9). Therefore, we must treat every
person—regardless of ethnicity, race, religion, or lifestyle—as
potential children.

> He died for everyone so that those who receive his new life will no
> longer live for themselves. Instead, they will live for Christ, who died
> and was raised for them. So we have stopped evaluating others from
> a human point of view. At one time we thought of Christ merely
> from a human point of view. How differently we know him now!
>
> 2 Corinthians 5:15–16 NLT

People of all faiths and backgrounds, colors, shapes, and sizes were planted in their mother's womb by a loving and gracious God, the only Creator in existence, the only One who has the power to make people and to save them—whether they acknowledge Him or not.

So until the day heaven takes over the earth, I don't see people as unbelievers. Only *pre*believers. And it's our privilege as Christians to show them why life with Christ is a good choice. Are we doing that? Are our actions, words, and opinions demonstrating a loving, accepting God? Our perspective shapes our witness. So we need to make sure the way we view people is aligned with the way God sees them.

Perspective Check #2—Christians Are One Body

Maybe you've got that whole witness thing down. You love prebelievers, you embrace them, you invite them over for fondue—that's great. That's awesome. But how are you doing at loving other Christians?

Recently I read a stack of survey replies about a church event I'd helped plan. Most of them were encouraging or constructive, but a few were shockingly mean. I tried to shrug them off, but it's hard to keep a handful of pepper from ruining the whole jar of honey.

The more I thought about it, though, I had to admit—haven't I been a speck of pepper before, too? Haven't you?

Anytime we gripe about our church, our leaders, or our sisters in Christ.

When the worship service is too loud, too slow, has too many hymns, not enough hymns, and why do they let that guy with the neck tattoos onto the stage? Don't we have standards here?

When the Bible study leader won't cut off the chatterbox sitting across from you, when the snack table has too many baked goods, not enough baked goods, when the book they chose is too fluffy or too serious, too short or too long. Who are "they," anyway? Can't "they" choose something better next time, for heaven's sake?

What if the preacher has too many bullet points, not enough bullet points, or no clear point at all? Don't we have a right to complain? To make sure the people in charge know they should work harder to meet our needs because, after all, they exist to serve? Yes, yes they do. They exist to serve—God. And so do you. So do I. It's a job we all share. That's why the Bible calls God's people the body of Christ.

> The human body has many parts, but the many parts make up one whole body. So it is with the body of Christ. . . . The eye can never say to the hand, "I don't need you." The head can't say to the feet, "I don't need you. . . ." If one part suffers, all the parts suffer with it, and if one part is honored, all the parts are glad.
>
> 1 Corinthians 12:12, 21, 26 NLT

Your pastor, your worship team, your Bible study leader, your Sunday school teacher, the mom sitting next to you with a screaming child, that college student with purple hair, and every single believer in your congregation—not to mention all other Christian congregations in the world—are a part of the same body. *Our* body. Which means when we swing our complaints like axes, ready to whack a foot because we don't like the way it's walking, we're actually chopping off our own foot.

Ouch.

In order to survive, a body needs all its parts working in harmony. And yes, sometimes that means we should get a checkup, a dose of medicine, or even surgery. That's what constructive criticism and accountability rooted in love can do for the body. That's healthy.

But there's a big difference between constructive criticism and self-serving complaints.

So next time you're tempted to hack a body part, ask yourself— what's my motive? We may be entitled to our own opinions, but nobody is entitled to chop the body to bits. If your intention is to build up the body, then by all means, offer your thoughts with a spirit of encouragement.

But if your words are just going to cut and sting, please remember, you're only hurting yourself—and God.

> But encourage one another daily, as long as it is called "Today," so that none of you may be hardened by sin's deceitfulness.
>
> Hebrews 3:13

Perspective Check #3—You Exist to Serve

Now, about that idea of servanthood. As we've just established, it's not meant exclusively for those in leadership or lowly positions. Serving is not a vocation; it's a state of heart.

> You, my brothers and sisters, were called to be free. But do not use your freedom to indulge the flesh; rather, serve one another humbly in love. For the entire law is fulfilled in keeping this one command: "Love your neighbor as yourself."
>
> Galatians 5:13

As Christians, we exist to love God and others. One major way we demonstrate our love is by serving. This requires fine-tuning our perspective toward people whose job—vocation—is to serve us. For example, is that gas station clerk standing behind the counter in order to serve you, or are you there to serve her?

Does your child's teacher arrive in the classroom every day to serve your family, or are you in a position to serve him?

Should your mail carrier, your waiter, your flight attendant, your contractor, your baby-sitter, your hygienist, your pizza delivery guy serve you only, or should you not also view your interactions with these people—God's created ones—as opportunities to serve *them*?

For even the Son of Man came not to be served but to serve others and to give his life as a ransom for many.

Matthew 20:28 NLT

Many of us are terribly prone to grumbling when a "servant" falls short of our needs. Perhaps instead we ought to consider how we can meet *their* needs. Smile at the tired Walmart cashier and ask how her day is going. Thank your barista and pray for her family. Write a note of encouragement to your child's soccer referee. Nobody's asking you to hang on a cross for these people. Jesus already did that for you and me *and* the referee. All we have to do is be kind.

So when the sin nature is tempted to demand, accuse, and complain, let's invoke God's wisdom and strength to serve a servant instead.

Wow. How might that shock the world for Jesus?

Perspective Check #4—Blessings Are Everywhere

We've already discussed how living "others first" requires keeping our eyes open to God's invitations. He brings us people to bless all the time; we just need to notice, and then act. But there's a flip side. We also need to recognize the blessings God gives *to us* every day.

Let all that I am praise the Lord; may I never forget the good things he does for me.

Psalm 103:2 NLT

It's easy to get wrapped up in all the crud that's going wrong in our lives. Bills, sickness, work stress, relationship struggles, you name it. We can get so focused on the mud on our shoes that we forget about the sunshine overhead.

Yet here's the crazy truth. When we see and receive God's blessings, we'll be more likely to *give* blessings. Why? Think of it this way: If you make a batch of fresh, gooey, delicious chocolate chip cookies, you might eat a few (or twelve) yourself, but chances are you'll also want to share them, right? God blessed you with the ingredients and the ability to make those cookies, and you're happy to give them to your kids, your co-workers, your guests. You love to see the smiles those cookies bring to people's faces. Cookies are wonderful! Let's all enjoy the cookies!

Blessings work quite the same way. The more we are blessed, the more we feel spurred to bless others. Which means that in order to love to our full potential, we need to realize just how very blessed we are to begin with.

Yes, the bills are due. But thank God for a home and heat and clean water. Even the mortgage and the energy bills are, on the flip side, a blessing.

I hate the stomach flu as much as any other girl. But thank God we live in a modern age of Pedialyte and OxiClean.

Relationships can be complicated and heart wrenching—and yet they teach us how to love flawed people like Jesus does. The hard stuff makes us more like Him. And that is a blessing indeed.

> Dear brothers and sisters, when troubles of any kind come your way, consider it an opportunity for great joy. For you know that when your faith is tested, your endurance has a chance to grow. So let it grow, for when your endurance is fully developed, you will be perfect and complete, needing nothing.
>
> James 1:2–4 NLT

I have wonderful friends. A great church. My husband is an excellent dad. So I may not have granite countertops, but my cupboard is full of food, and I can pack a healthy lunch for my amazing kids on a laminate surface just as well as I could on that elusive remodeled kitchen. Who needs it? I have so much already.

What about you? What are your blessings? Have you been counting them lately? Or, like I do sometimes, are you allowing grievances to overshadow your gratitude?

Proverbs 4:23 says, "Above all else, guard your heart, for everything you do flows from it." Part of "guarding your heart" involves filling it with the right perspective. Recognize your blessings. Praise God for them. Let them soak your heart with thankfulness, so that when it's touched and squeezed by another person's need, God's love can't help but pour out.

Perspective Check #5—Keep an Eternal Outlook

Our final perspective check is arguably the most important of all. No matter what challenges you may go through in your relationships, your responsibilities, your burdens—remember this: All our trials on earth are temporary. God is working now to restore our lives for eternity. And eternity lasts a lot longer than today.

Remember my friend Valerie? She's counting on that:

"I truly believe all the problems I'm going through in my relationships right now is just the fertilizer for the relationships I will cultivate in heaven. When people hurt us and we feel like we can't repair what's broken, we need to step back and see the bigger picture—the eternal perspective—or we're just going to despair. My struggles here are preparing my eternal garden for harvest. I really believe that one day, when all is made perfect again, those relationships will be beautiful."

> Therefore, since we are surrounded by such a great cloud of witnesses, let us throw off everything that hinders and the sin that so easily entangles. And let us run with perseverance the race marked out for us, fixing our eyes on Jesus, the pioneer and perfecter of faith. For the joy set before him he endured the cross, scorning its shame, and sat down at the right hand of the throne of God. Consider him who endured such opposition from sinners, so that you will not grow weary and lose heart.
>
> Hebrews 12:1–3

──────── **Let's Dig Deeper** ────────

1. Review the five perspective checks outlined in this chapter:

   • People belong to God
   • Christians are one body
   • You exist to serve
   • Blessings are everywhere
   • Keep an eternal outlook

   Did any of these open your eyes to a blind spot? Which perspective check impacted you most, and why?

2. Read 2 Corinthians 5:20–21. What does it mean to be an ambassador for Christ? How does the way we view people affect how well we represent the gospel to others (especially prebelievers)?

3. Have you ever harbored a grievance against your church or fellowship group? What is the difference between complaining and constructive criticism? How does perspective check #2 affect the way you view your grievances?

4. Are you quick to point out other people's flaws? Read Psalm 139:24 and Matthew 7:3–5. What do these verses suggest we should focus on instead?

5. Recall our Blessing Toolbox from chapter 4. One of our tools is to be a cheerleader. Read Ephesians 4:29. Why are encouraging words vital to building others up? Conversely, how can hurtful words tear others down? What does this do to the body of Christ?

6. Serving others requires cultivating a spirit of humility. What keeps you from being humble?

7. Read 1 Thessalonians 5:16–18. How can giving thanks help us maintain sight of our blessings? What role does prayer play in developing a sense of gratitude?

8. How can an eternal perspective comfort us in our troubles? See Romans 8:28; Genesis 50:20; Jeremiah 29:11; Lamentations 3:58; John 16:33; and 2 Corinthians 4:16–18.

Love in Motion

Next time you go to a store checkout or restaurant, imagine you are there to serve the servant. Offer some form of blessing to the cashier or wait staff—a warm greeting, genuine conversation, asking how you can pray for them, etc. Choose to see that person as someone God has asked you to influence for Him. How does this affect your behavior? Your attitude? Your mood?

— Chapter 10 —

Loving People
Who Aren't Like You

My senior pastor, Dennis Episcopo, is a straight-talking Italian from New York City. From the pulpit and in daily life, he is wise, impassioned, and zealous for the lost.

Did I mention he is wise?

Yes. Wise enough to recognize his own flubs.

I was waiting in line at the department store, and there's this girl standing ahead of me. She's all tatted up, and she's got piercings all over her face, including one in her tongue. You could see it because she opened her mouth to start chatting with other customers in line. I stood there looking at her, tapping my toes, thinking, *C'mon, you're slowing things down. Other people have schedules, for crying out loud.* She was so patient and polite to the other people in line, but the whole time I'm just getting more impatient and ticked off. Then all of a sudden she turns around and sees me. She gets this look of shock on her face and says, "Pastor! It's so good to see you! Great sermon on Sunday. Wow, that one really made an impact on me!" And I tell you what—I was cut to the quick. It was like

God was shouting at me, *When are you gonna learn not to judge people on the outside?*

Not a single one of us is immune to misperceptions. We can quickly size up a person and make assumptions about who they are or what they believe, based on—what? Their clothing? Their skin color? Their occupation, their mannerisms, their politics, the car they drive, the food they eat, their favorite sports team? I live in Green Bay Packer country, and I'm telling you, yes, it takes a certain special variety of person to willingly wear a foam cheese hat in public, but even this does not denote the specifics of the super fan's character. Some of them are actually pretty normal people Monday through Saturday.

Shallow, external judgment is dangerous. Because, as Pastor Dennis says, it destroys the work of God.

"When you make judgments based on appearances, you're not in a position to be salt and light and to love people," he explained. "You're out of play! You can't be used in a redemptive way because you're not focused on their heart; you're focused on your opinions and your prejudices. Not to mention, you're wrong most of the time."

Bottom line? If you want to be used by the Master, look beyond appearances. Get to know where people are coming from and how their life story has shaped them. Be open, be kind. And understand that different does not automatically mean wrong.

And may the Lord make your love for one another *and for all people* grow and overflow, just as our love for you overflows.

1 Thessalonians 3:12 NLT, emphasis added

Live Like Kingdom Subjects

I love my book club friends. We meet once a month to examine a chosen novel's storyline, characters, symbolism, intentions. Ooh, I just love to pick apart a good book. Our group discussions are intellectual, creative, amiable, and intense. They stimulate my brain and warm my heart. Plus somebody usually bakes a great quiche or coffee cake. Score.

When it comes down to the big question at the end of each meeting—did you like the book?—not all of us agree. But on most other significant issues, we do.

We're all Christians. We're all moms. We're all Wisconsinites with laundry to fold and husbands to feed. We can talk about foreshadowing and point of view, switch the topic to school bus routes, and back again without missing a beat.

It's easy to love these ladies. They're a lot like me. So what about people who aren't?

> If all you do is love the lovable, do you expect a bonus? Anybody can do that. If you simply say hello to those who greet you, do you expect a medal? Any run-of-the-mill sinner does that. In a word, what I'm saying is, *Grow up*. You're kingdom subjects. Now live like it. Live out your God-created identity. Live generously and graciously toward others, the way God lives toward you.
>
> Matthew 5:46–48 THE MESSAGE

Ouch.

Grow up. Those were Jesus' words. Okay, so maybe *The Message* version borders on slang, but the impact is accurate. Basically Jesus is saying, *Hey, what makes you think you're being like me if you're only friendly to your friends?*

Jesus hung out with a lot of questionable characters. Tax collectors (scoundrels), prostitutes (loose women), fishermen (blue collars), Samaritans (liberals).

We label people, don't we? Yet Jesus is saying people are not categories. They're not stereotypes. They're people. So treat them the way God would.

Love them.

> Here's another way to put it: You're here to be light, bringing out the God-colors in the world. . . . Keep open house; be generous

with your lives. By opening up to others, you'll prompt people to open up with God, this generous Father in heaven.

Matthew 5:14, 16 THE MESSAGE

What Would Jesus Do?

Brian and Amy text each other daily. Brian visits Amy's house, plays with her kids, and gives her a ride to work when her car breaks down. They're close friends. Actually, Amy says, they're like family.

You'd never guess that just three months ago, Brian and Amy were total strangers.

"I sent him a message by accident," Amy said. "And it all escalated from there."

A single mom of three children, Amy was struggling to manage life's demands. She had recently moved across state lines and had no close friends or family nearby to depend on. When her kids went through a spell of colds and flu, she missed too much work and lost her job. With no income, no home, and no car, she reached out in desperation to an acquaintance on Facebook.

"Wondering if you know a good Bible verse for someone to pray when in deep fear, weak, and personal despair?"

The moment she hit Send, Amy realized her mistake. She meant to send the plea to someone of a similar name, but it went instead to Brian—a stranger. She quickly retracted. "Wrong person, I am so sorry."

Brian disagreed.

"God puts people in our lives for a reason," he said. Brian sent Amy several Bible verses, but he didn't stop there. "The one question that kept rolling through my mind was—what would Jesus do?" So he drove to the hotel where Amy and her children were staying and paid for a two-nights' stay. Then he helped Amy set up a charitable funding page, where donations began flooding in. Within a few short days, Amy had enough money to get back on her feet. Someone lent her a car. Another person connected her to a new job opportunity. Today she is working full-time as a nurse and providing for her kids as best she can.

"Brian continues to check in on me all the time," she said. "It's been amazing having him in my life. He's the kind of friend who speaks truth and holds me accountable. He loves me but he's not afraid to scold me when I need it, and I appreciate him for that. All of this has restored my faith in humanity. It has restored my faith in God."

Brian wasn't looking for a friend. He wasn't looking for another responsibility. He couldn't relate directly to Amy's life circumstances or struggles. They had practically nothing in common. But he saw an opportunity to bless someone, and he acted on it. Why? *Because doing so honors God.*

> "I was hungry, and you gave me something to eat. I was thirsty, and you gave me something to drink. I was a stranger, and you took me into your home. I needed clothes, and you gave me something to wear. I was sick, and you took care of me. I was in prison, and you visited me." Then the people who have God's approval will reply to him, "Lord, when did we see you hungry and feed you or see you thirsty and give you something to drink? When did we see you as a stranger and take you into our homes or see you in need of clothes and give you something to wear? When did we see you sick or in prison and visit you?" The king will answer them, "I can guarantee this truth: Whatever you did for one of my brothers or sisters, no matter how unimportant they seemed, you did for me."
>
> Matthew 25:35–40 GW

The Way to a Woman's Heart

Wendi is a mom, teacher, and camp counselor; she loves Jesus and her husband and her church. Oh, and she visits strip clubs on a regular basis.

Not to work. She goes there to serve.

And to make friends.

Wendi is involved in a ministry called Sweet Treats, an outreach designed to bring God's love to dark places. Each week, Wendi and a team of fellow volunteers deliver baskets of baked goods and toiletries to venues where women work as exotic dancers. They go with the intention of building relationships and spreading joy. Ultimately their hope is to introduce the women to Jesus, but make no mistake—Sweet Treats is not just an end-goal ministry. The volunteers are invested long-term. They offer their time, attention, prayers, and authentic friendship to the women they serve, because they believe they're worth it.

"These friends live very different lives from us," Wendi explained. "They've told us that when we visit, they feel like 'normal people' because we are willing to come into their world and talk as friends who respect them and honor their personhood."

Wendi never refers to the women as strippers or dancers. She doesn't even call them women. They are always and simply *friends*.

"One dear friend came into work with a cup from the coffee shop and another friend asked her what she got and if she had gone to the drive-thru," Wendi recalled. "She stated emphatically that when she gets coffee in town, she *never* goes through the drive-thru, because when she goes inside the shop, she loves to just look around at all the people drinking coffee and on their computers and chatting and reading, and she pretends that for a moment, she is just like them."

Although the Sweet Treats friends feel separated from the rest of the world, Wendi does what she can to bridge the gap. Many of the friends are also mothers, so they find common ground in talking about their kids. In one case Wendi planned a playdate to a local splash pad with a friend and her children.

"After we set the date," Wendi said, "she looked at me and said, 'Huh. So I guess I have a real friend now?'"

Although this friend has since finished her nursing degree and left the dancing scene, the two women stay in touch. "I hope she knows she is worthy of real friendship," Wendi said. "And she still has one in me."

Jesus had a tender heart toward lost and troubled people. Just look at the Gospels and you'll see He absolved an adulteress from stoning (John 8:2–11), offered living water to a gal cohabitating out of wedlock (John 4:1–26), and allowed a disgraced woman to wash His feet with her tears (Luke 7:36–50). He didn't enable them, but He forgave them. He valued them. He redirected them. He *loved* them.

How much? The Bible can answer that.

> You see, at just the right time, when we were still powerless, Christ died for the ungodly. Very rarely will anyone die for a righteous person, though for a good person someone might possibly dare to die. But God demonstrates his own love for us in this: While we were still sinners, Christ died for us.
>
> Romans 5:6–8

Put Yourself in Their Shoes

If you've ever traveled to a country that doesn't speak your language or share your climate or drive on your side of the road, you know firsthand how difficult it is to be an outsider. Navigating strange territory is a vulnerable task.

Ib discovered this the first week she arrived in Canada.

A native of Nigeria, Ib (pronounced EYE-bee) is a highly educated woman, devoted wife, and mom of two young boys. When her husband was offered an opportunity to live and work in Ontario, the entire family packed minimal belongings and relocated halfway across the world.

"Initially I thought we wouldn't need any help," she said. "I thought we could throw money at whatever we wanted and it would be okay."

It wasn't.

First the couple learned they couldn't buy a house. They came to Canada with plenty of cash in hand, but the banks required a half year of credit history. So did rental properties, which meant in order to obtain an apartment, Ib's family had to pay five months of rent up front. That ate a chunk of what they had for starters. Thankfully they were able to purchase furniture, but learned it would take six weeks to build and deliver their order. And to top it all off, Ib's husband traveled off shore for work, leaving her home alone with their boys for weeks at a time—in an unfamiliar country, with no car and no relatives nearby.

"Here it was coming up on Christmas, and we were lonely and missing our support system," Ib explained. They decided extras weren't a necessity under the circumstances, so they held off on buying a Christmas tree and chose just one gift for each of the boys. "We figured we'd just enjoy our family and get through this difficult time on our own," she said.

But then a neighbor stopped by and noticed their apartment was bare. She called Ib the next day. "I hope you don't mind," she told her, "but a friend of mine is moving, and she has no need for her table and chairs. She'll deliver them tomorrow, along with a bed."

Then at school drop-off one morning, a fellow mom asked Ib how they were settling in. "She asked me if I was going to put up a Christmas tree, and I explained why we weren't," Ib said. "So she told me she'd just gotten a new artificial tree and would be happy to give us her old one. The offer was so genuine and out of the blue—I was really touched."

But that's not all. This new mom friend took Ib shopping for her boys' Christmas gifts and drove all across town to find the best price. Another woman gifted Ib money to buy tree lights. Then someone left a bag of presents on her doorstep two days before Christmas, signed "Your Secret Santa." Blessings poured in, unsolicited, from neighbors and fellow school parents who recognized an opportunity to help make one family's cross-cultural transition easier.

"They really helped ease a lot of the pain," Ib said. "But more than that, they opened my eyes to the beauty of blessing others."

Ib asked herself, *How have I gone out of my way for someone else when I didn't even know what pain they were going through?* And she couldn't remember. Most of the people she'd helped in Nigeria would actually come ask her for help. "In my case, though, I was too self-sufficient to ask for the help, but they offered it anyway," Ib said. "This is a wake-up call that where you are needed, you don't always need to hear it for you to know. You just need to put yourself in the other person's shoes."

Since then, Ib has done just that. She began looking for opportunities to bless people, starting with a neighbor who had just given birth to her second child. "I know how it is, having to be up all night with both kids," Ib said. "So I do the dishes, I watch the children while she takes a nap."

Out of gratitude, her neighbor's husband gave Christmas gifts to Ib's boys—evidence of how one blessing propels another and then another. These were different people, raised on different continents, with different needs and burdens. Yet they all chose to see each other as God's loved ones—worthy of respect and care.

"We may reach a point of comfort in our Christian lives where we lose sight of God's nudges," Ib said. "But I want to have full dependence on God. No more 'I know how to' but rather, 'Lord, show me.'"

Show me. That's my hope for us all. That God would give us the right perspective, to help us see people and needs and opportunities the way He sees them.

They're everywhere. And they're beautiful.

Don't you have a saying, "It's still four months until harvest"? I tell you, open your eyes and look at the fields! They are ripe for harvest.

John 4:35

50 Ways to Bless with Your Perspective

1. Smile at people!
2. Say hello to newcomers at work, school, or elsewhere. Look them in the eye.
3. Encourage your children's God-given personality and interests.
4. Strike up a conversation at church with someone you don't know well. Ask questions and listen to the answers.
5. Give compliments. Simple comments such as "Those jeans look cute on you!" or "Your hair looks so pretty today" can boost a person's mood in seconds.
6. When you see a mom struggling in public with unruly kids, tell her she's a great mom.
7. Brag on someone else's child.
8. Share your personal testimony of how you came to know the Lord.
9. Pray for bad drivers who cut you off in traffic. You have no idea what's going on in their car at the moment, or what kind of day they're having.
10. Ask your teen son or daughter to share their favorite music or book. Ask questions about it. Resist the urge to criticize.
11. Invite the new family in your neighborhood/church/school over for dinner.
12. Take an interest in a younger employee at work. Offer to take her to lunch and ask questions about her background and interests.
13. Encourage your child to befriend the "loner."
14. Take a godly woman's advice.
15. Offer godly advice when someone asks you for it.
16. Answer your child's endless questions, rather than getting annoyed by them. You were once an inquisitive child, too. (See Matthew 19:14.)

17. Give a hug to someone who's crying.
18. Thank your husband for the work he does around the house.
19. Encourage co-workers with your positive attitude. Remember you're working for the Lord, not for human masters (Colossians 3:23).
20. Forgive someone.
21. Give the benefit of the doubt.
22. Welcome an interruption as part of God's plan for your day.
23. Pray for your enemies. Remember God loves them.
24. Walk away from gossip. Or, if appropriate, defend the person being gossiped about.
25. Ask an elderly person about her favorite memories. Remember you, too, will one day grow old.
26. Be friendly to service people. Look them in the eye, ask them how their day is going. Thank them for the work they do.
27. Tell your children you love them—when they're in the middle of a snit.
28. Host a multicultural dinner at your home or church. Invite people of all backgrounds to contribute recipes from their native cultures.
29. Ask a refugee family to share their story at your small group meeting.
30. Affirm the women's retreat or summer camp coordinator. Tell her you appreciate her hard work.
31. Thank your mother-in-law for raising a great son.
32. Welcome your child's teen friends into your home. Get to know them. Be a safe place.
33. Refrain from responding to insults with more insults.
34. When you're tempted to point out someone else's flaws, pray instead for God to help you recognize your own.

35. If you have non-English speakers in your church or neighborhood, learn to say a few key phrases in their native language. Greet them with a translated "hello."

36. Host a foreign exchange student.

37. Don't believe everything you read or see in the media. Filter all news through Scripture.

38. Love on divorced people.

39. Pray privately for brothers and sisters in Christ who are struggling with addiction, pornography, adultery, or abuse. If a close friend is affected by these strongholds, be her sounding board and offer accountability.

40. Seek out a prebeliever and invite her out for coffee.

41. Practice seeing people as souls, not bodies.

42. Welcome strangers into your church. Offer to show them around.

43. Shake people's hands.

44. If your pastor's sermon encouraged you or taught you something new, tell him so. Thank him for his preparation, wisdom, and insight.

45. Don't allow church groups to become cliques. On Sundays or in your small group meeting, sit next to someone new, someone unfriendly, or someone others may ostracize. Demonstrate the love of Christ through genuine friendliness. (The same applies to your workplace, your moms' group, your parent-teacher association, etc.)

46. Applaud the opposing team—win or lose.

47. Prepare vegetarian, sugar-free, or gluten-free options for a potluck.

48. Do not shame your spouse, friend, or child for having an opinion different from yours. Remember that in areas of personal (not biblical) conviction, *different* does not necessarily mean *wrong*.

49. Make grace your default response to everything and everyone.

50. Count your own blessings.

——— **Let's Dig Deeper** ———

1. Consider Pastor Dennis's story again about waiting in line. Have you ever had a similar experience in which you were quick to criticize someone because of their outward appearance? What motives were behind your judgment? Pride? Fear? Entitlement? Other?

2. Judging by appearances can also involve admiring someone undeservedly. Read James 2:1–5. What external features may cause you to assess a person as "good"? How can this form of external judgment be just as dangerous as condemnation?

3. Review Matthew 5:46–48. Are you only friendly to your friends? If so, how does this hinder your witness for Christ?

4. Read Colossians 4:5–6. Who are your "outsiders," as the NIV puts it? How can cultivating a lifestyle of blessing help you "make the most of every opportunity"?

5. What did you think of Amy and Brian's story? Did it encourage you or convict you? Why?

6. In Matthew 25:40, Jesus says, "Truly I tell you, whatever you did for one of the least of these brothers and sisters of mine, you did for me." How should this truth affect the way we look at "lesser" people?

7. Consider Ib's story. When was the last time you put yourself in someone else's shoes? How could developing that type of perspective help you bless others more effectively?

8. John 4:35 says, "Open your eyes and look at the fields!" Where are your "fields"? Why do you think Jesus wants us to see that they are ripe for the harvest? What kind of action is He calling for in this passage?

Love in Motion

"Open your eyes" and identify a person or need that could benefit from your blessing. Then choose one or more of the "50 Ways to Bless with Your Perspective," and *do it*.

Chapter 11

Four P's of Blessing
#4 Prayer

My friend Rachel is vibrant, lovely, and wise. She is a seminary graduate, passionate about God's Word, the devoted wife of an equally devoted husband, keeper of a spacious and charming yellow house—her dream home. From the outside you'd think she has it all. And she does. She has Christ—her all in all.

She is painfully aware of how much she needs Him.

Rachel learned the hard way how to cling to God—through suffering. It all began four years ago, when she was just twenty-nine.

"Something didn't feel quite right," she said. "We were moving into our new house, and my energy started to fail. Suddenly I found myself getting easily fatigued by the simplest tasks."

Over the next few weeks, Rachel's knees began to swell until they reached the size of cantaloupes. As the swelling increased, the pain grew. "It hurt to walk, it hurt to stand, it hurt to move."

Rachel lost twenty-five pounds and became confined to her couch, without even enough energy to make herself a sandwich. Simply hobbling across the floor to the bathroom became a tremendous feat. Test after test came back normal; doctors could find no explanation for her symptoms.

"My body was rapidly breaking down before my very eyes," she remembers, "and there was nothing I could do about it."

For several months, Rachel's once-active days became controlled by severe exhaustion, deficient memory, insomnia, night sweats, and debilitating inflammation. She cried out to God, "Lord, do you see? Do you care? Why haven't you healed me? Will this ever end?" And she heard no answers.

Until one day, a card showed up in her mailbox.

Dear Rachel—You don't know me at all, but I have been praying deeply for you. In fact, your name is taped on my bathroom mirror. Please remember that your name is inscribed in the palm of His hand. May He cover you with a blanket of His love.

And then another.

Precious one, you've been in a long battle; please tie a knot and hang on!

And another.

Your name is on our minds, hearts, and lips as we are earnestly praying for a return to good health for you. Jesus loves and cares for you so much. May He give you healing and peace of mind.

Soon she was flooded with cards and letters from unfamiliar names and street addresses, each one postmarked Ontario, Ohio— her grandparents' hometown.

"My grandparents had asked their church to pray for me," she said. "Just when I had lost the strength to pray for myself, all of these sweet people, my grandparents' friends and fellow congregation members whom I'd never met, were encouraging me and lifting me up in their prayers daily. The fact that God would put my name on the hearts of so many strangers became a tangible reminder of His love and grace in the midst of a challenging situation. It gave me hope that I was not alone in it."

Word spread until four churches in Ohio were praying fervently for Rachel's health. These strangers became her intercessors. They conveyed the voice of God. They reminded her that God *did* see, He *did* hear. He was *with her* through every excruciating ache and worry. Ultimately, the prayers of God's people not only blessed Rachel with encouragement, they also drew her nearer to the Lord.

> The Lord is close to all who call on him, yes, to all who call on him in truth. He grants the desires of those who fear him; he hears their cries for help and rescues them.
>
> Psalm 145:18–19 NLT

Our final and perhaps most important P is prayer. Pleading to God on behalf of another person, asking Him to heal, equip, provide, or protect—these are the kind of blessings that, more than any other, directly summon the power and promises of God. In this chapter and the next, we're going to examine how prayer can make a tremendous impact on individual people and the kingdom as a whole. As Christians, we're not only called to pray; it is our privilege to do so.

> Let us then approach God's throne of grace with confidence, so that we may receive mercy and find grace to help us in our time of need.
>
> Hebrews 4:16

Why Pray for Others?

Sometimes I think my prayers sound like a grocery list. "Lord, please bring me lots of blessings. I need safety for our trip to Chicago and money to fix that noise in my brakes. Plus, hey, Jesus, please heal me from this annoying cough before Friday because I've got a really busy weekend coming up, 'kay? Thanks so much!"

I mean, the Bible does tell us to pray often and for every little thing, right? We're supposed to "pray continually" (1 Thessalonians 5:17) and "pray about everything" (Philippians 4:6 NLT). So I do. I ask God to check off the list of things that will fill my cupboard and satisfy my belly. And then I top it all off with a holy little "your will be done!" because that's what faith-filled Christians do.

But is that all we do?

If your prayer life consists primarily of requests for yourself, like mine sometimes does, then we're both missing a tremendous opportunity to participate in God's amazing work on earth.

> Therefore confess your sins to each other and pray for each other so that you may be healed. *The prayer of a righteous person is powerful and effective.*
>
> James 5:16, emphasis added

Wow. The Bible says prayer is powerful. It's effective, or, as another translation puts it, prayer "produces wonderful results" (NLT). Well . . . of course it does! Prayer is conversation with God, the Creator of the Universe, the One who knows everything and sees everything and can do anything. Prayer is not a passive habit or something to grasp as a last resort. Prayer is mighty. Prayer is action.

And sister, don't be afraid of that word *righteous*. You and I may not be perfect, but we are justified in Christ, which makes us righteous people in God's eyes. You have every right to call on the name of the Lord in prayer.

> Because of Christ and our faith in him, we can now come boldly and confidently into God's presence.
>
> Ephesians 3:12 NLT

Now don't get me wrong—praying for ourselves is a good thing. God wants us to share our inmost hearts with Him, of course. Even

Jesus, just hours before the crucifixion, prayed for the Father to "take this cup of suffering away from me" (Luke 22:42 NLT).

But prayer can also be so much more. As Christians we want to be like Christ, right? Isn't that the goal? Then we need to dig into the Gospels and discover how Jesus really prayed. He didn't just send up requests for himself. He interceded for others. He prayed fervently for friends and sinners. He committed them to the Father for their benefit and blessing. Therefore, as Christ's followers, we, too, ought to be on holy fire to pray for people and situations beyond ourselves.

> After saying all these things, Jesus looked up to heaven and said, "Father, the hour has come. Glorify your Son so he can give glory back to you. . . . My prayer is . . . for those you have given me, because they belong to you. . . . Now I am departing from the world; they are staying in this world, but I am coming to you. Holy Father, you have given me your name; now protect them by the power of your name so that they will be united just as we are. . . . I am praying not only for these disciples but also for all who will ever believe in me through their message."
>
> John 17:1, 9, 11, 20 NLT

Prayer—the Cliffs' Notes

I confess that for me, prayer is one of the most confusing aspects of the Christian life. I've asked many questions over the years, like, how does God hear all of us at once? Why does He say no to "good" requests? If God is sovereign, then what difference do my prayers make? Isn't He just going to do what He wants anyway?

Do you wonder, too? I've done a lot of research on the topic of prayer, and I know I'm still only scratching the surface. Yet I believe I can offer a few overarching truths from Scripture that will settle your questions well enough to give this fourth P an even chance.

Does God Really Hear My Prayers?

Yes. It's wild, isn't it? Our sovereign God, the Creator of every-thing and everyone, is at this very moment holding the entire universe in balance—and yet He has the time and the patience and the desire to listen to each one of His children when they call on Him. How do I know? The Bible says so. Over and over and over again.

> The eyes of the Lord are on the righteous, and his ears are attentive to their cry.
>
> Psalm 34:15

Why Should I Pray When God Already Knows My Needs?

Ah. Prayer is not for God so much as it is for *you*. Yes, He already knows what you need. You don't need to inform Him. But He likes to hear from you. He's crazy about you. He wants a relationship with you. James 4:2 says, "You do not have because you do not ask God." So for heaven's sake, *ask* already. Cultivating a lifestyle of communication with God will only help you grow stronger spiritu-ally, emotionally, and relationally. And when we bring our needs before God, we are reminded that He is in control.

> God is our refuge and strength, an ever-present help in trouble.
>
> Psalm 46:1

Why Doesn't God Always Give Me What I Ask for?

I heard a pastor tell an analogy of a toddler who begs to play with the hair dryer—in the bathtub. Um, no parent in her right mind is going to say "Sure!" to that electrifying request. And it's the same with God. He is our Perfect Parent. He will never give us anything that is not somehow part of His good plan for us. So sometimes we may ask for something that we're certain, in our limited understanding, is good, but God knows it's not—or at least not right now. As Garth Brooks says, some of God's greatest gifts are unanswered prayers. Amen to that.

Does Prayer Change God's Mind?

No. God knows His mind; it's flawless and all-knowing and pure, and He certainly doesn't need us to sway His wisdom or convictions. Nor is He reluctant to answer us, as though a little human coaxing will make the difference. God is unchangeable (Malachi 3:6; James 1:17; Hebrews 13:8; 1 Samuel 15:29). Therefore, prayer does not change God; it just stakes a claim on His will. Like we saw in James 4:2, God may already know what He is willing (even eager!) to give us or do for us, but sometimes our decision to ask for it, as a demonstration of our faith, is what triggers God to act.

How Can I Know What God's Will Is?

God's will is a bit of a mystery. We can know basic right from wrong; the Bible is filled with guidance on what God finds acceptable and what He doesn't. Yet even within those parameters there's a lot of detail in God's plan for our lives that we can't possibly comprehend. Romans 11:34 says, "For who can know the Lord's thoughts? Who knows enough to give him advice?" (NLT). Basically we are like tiny ant brains compared to the wisdom and majesty of God.

And yet, Psalm 37:4 says, "Take delight in the Lord, and he will give you the desires of your heart." This suggests that the more we delight in God—the more we get to know Him and love Him and remain closely connected to Him—the more likely our desires will line up with His desires for us. That's a pretty cool promise.

One of the best explanations I've heard on the question of praying for God's will came from Dr. Adrian Rogers:

The prayer that gets to heaven is the prayer that starts in heaven. We just close the circuit. The will of God is what you would want if you knew everything from God's viewpoint. The key is to abide in Christ. If you abide in Him (John 15:7), you will find that God will guide and direct your prayers, and you will be praying in the will of God. Don't wait until you have all of the answers before you pray. You don't have to understand electricity to turn on the lights.[1]

Is There a "Right" Way to Pray?

Prayer is simply conversation with God. It should be authentic and from the heart; beyond that, there's lots of wiggle room. However, Jesus did give us a helpful model in the Gospels. You and I may know it as the Our Father or the Lord's Prayer.

> This, then, is how you should pray: "Our Father in heaven, hallowed be your name, your kingdom come, your will be done, on earth as it is in heaven. Give us today our daily bread. And forgive us our debts, as we also have forgiven our debtors. And lead us not into temptation, but deliver us from the evil one."
>
> Matthew 6:9–13

Understand that this prayer was never meant to be droned. Jesus warns us not to "heap up empty phrases" when we pray (Matthew 6:7 ESV). Rather, the Lord's Prayer is a pattern for expressing our own words and concerns. From this passage, we can glean a few guidelines:

- Start by praising or thanking God
- Pray for His will to be done
- Ask for what you need
- Ask for forgiveness, and forgive any grudges you're holding
- Pray for God to guard your heart

Finally, John 14:13 says, "And I will do whatever you ask in my name, so that the Father may be glorified in the Son." When we call on Jesus, the name above all names (Philippians 2:9), we honor God and beseech the power of the holy Trinity. There is such potency in our prayers! So offer them up "in Jesus' name," amen.

Do's and Don'ts of Blessing with Prayer

Since prayer is a personal conversation between you and God, there is no real right or wrong. But if you want to effectively bless people with your prayers, I can offer a few suggestions.

DO pray in the moment.

Have you ever heard somebody say, "I'll pray for you!" and then the second they turn away, you just *know* they're never going to utter a single syllable about you to the Lord, those hypocrites! Ah, but aren't we all prone to it? I'm surrounded by so many friends and prayer needs on a daily basis, it can get tricky to keep track of it all.

So why delay? Sometimes the greatest blessing we can bestow on another person is to stop and pray *in the moment*. Lay your hand on a friend's shoulder and pray for her. Stop in the middle of your phone conversation to call upon the Lord together. Pray for the need you just read about in an email—*before* you swipe off your phone. Then instead of promising, "I'll pray for you," tell your sisters and brothers in Christ, "I *prayed* for you." And mean it.

DO pray Scripture.

God's Word is "alive and active" (Hebrews 4:12). It helps guide and train us. It encourages us. So include Scripture in your prayers for others. For example, "Lord, help my children to 'be strong and courageous,' and please be with them wherever they go" (from Joshua 1:9). When we use God's own words in our prayers back to Him, we not only pray according to God's will, we also lay claim to the promises of God.

As the rain and the snow come down from heaven, and do not return to it without watering the earth and making it bud and flourish, so that it yields seed for the sower and bread for the eater, so is my word that goes out from my mouth: It will not return to me empty, but will accomplish what I desire and achieve the purpose for which I sent it.

Isaiah 55:10–11

DO *pray for anything and everything.*

Some people need healing. Some people need to find their car keys. Believe it or not, God cares about both issues. One Bible commentary says, "It is the little cares of life that wear the heart out."[2] So don't try to weigh whether or not a need is "worthy" of God's attention. Bring it all to Him—big and small.

Do not be anxious about anything, but *in every situation*, by prayer and petition, with thanksgiving, present your requests to God.

Philippians 4:6, emphasis added

DON'T *scold or shame others with your prayers.*

Speaking of praying for anything, I recall standing in a circle with a group of musicians one morning, praying as we prepared to lead worship for a big church event. I was suffering from a minor health issue and asked for prayer that it wouldn't distract me from serving well. A few kind friends lifted this and other requests up to the Lord, but then one of my fellow musicians broke in with this prayer: "Lord, help us not to pray for insignificant things like health issues. Help us to see you are bigger than that."

Uh. What?

Was that a slam?

I think it was.

Perhaps he was just trying to inspire us to his higher plane of faith. But at that moment what I heard was, *Lord, tell Becky to get over herself.*

140

Please don't use prayer to scold or shame other people, especially in a group setting. Understand that we are all on a personal journey with the Lord, and He may be convicting us each of different lessons at different times. So use your prayers not as a soapbox but rather to "encourage one another and build each other up" (1 Thessalonians 5:11).

DON'T use prayer as a form of gossip.

Yes, you may be aware that your friend is cheating on her husband or your nephew is headed to rehab. But if this information was shared with you in confidence, please tread very cautiously. When a loved one is struggling with a private issue, they need support and accountability from people they trust. Let them determine who those people are. Asking unrelated parties to pray for someone else's embarrassing heartache doesn't *bless* anybody; it only exposes them to more hurt.

> Let no corrupting talk come out of your mouths, but only such as is good for building up, as fits the occasion, that it may give grace to those who hear.
>
> Ephesians 4:29 ESV

What Prayer Can Do

Remember all those cards Rachel received in her mailbox? I'd like to tell you how things turned out for her. Within a span of just a couple weeks, she collected more than eighty greetings, letters, poems, hymns, and Scripture passages—all sent from various prayer warriors in Ohio. She read every word, treasured every signature and story, and saved every note. Several months later, after countless doctors and tests, God answered their prayers. Rachel was diagnosed with an autoimmune disease—and given treatment. Within twenty-four hours of the first dose, her pain and swelling began to subside. God has now restored my sweet friend's quality of life.

Rachel reminded me of a story in Exodus 17, where the Israelites are in battle against an enemy army. Moses holds a staff up in his hands, and as long as he keeps it there, the Israelite army is winning. But he gets tired. He struggles to keep his hands held in the air. So Aaron and Hur go to Moses and stand at his sides, and they hold his arms up for him until the battle is won. "*That* is what these people did for me," Rachel explained. "That is the power of prayer. Through their prayers, these people held me up in a way that impacted my faith and gave me the ability to endure."

You want to bless somebody? Pray for them. God will do the rest.

I urge you, first of all, to pray for all people. Ask God to help them; intercede on their behalf, and give thanks for them.

1 Timothy 2:1 NLT

──────── **Let's Dig Deeper** ────────

1. Have you ever wondered whether or not God is listening? Look up the following verses: Jeremiah 29:12; 1 John 5:14–15; Matthew 21:22; Psalm 145:18; Revelation 3:20. What do these say about God's attentiveness to your prayers?

2. Study Psalm 66:17–20; 1 Peter 3:12; Isaiah 1:15; and Proverbs 28:9. How does sin hinder your communication with God? Yes, we are all sinners, but there is a difference between growing in your faith through stumbles (Philippians 2:12) and deliberately choosing to hold on to sin. One desires the things of God; the other does not. Where do you stand?

3. What is the role of confession in restoring our communication with God? See 1 John 1:9. Consider how this supports

the idea that we ought to ask for forgiveness as a regular part of our prayer life. (See our discussion of the Lord's Prayer in this chapter.)

4. Do you regularly pray for others? Why or why not?

5. Have you ever heard somebody say, "Well, I guess all we can do now is pray"? Do you view prayer as a last resort or a first step? Why?

6. Sometimes God says no to our prayers because we're asking for the wrong thing. See Numbers 11:11–15; Matthew 20:20–22; and James 4:3. What do these verses tell you about God's wisdom in responding to our prayers?

7. Have you ever received the blessing of someone else's prayers on your behalf? What was the result? How did this encourage you?

8. Do you believe God is able to answer your prayers? Read Luke 1:37 and Ephesians 3:20. What does the Bible say God is able to do?

Love in Motion

Ephesians 6:18 says, "And pray in the Spirit on all occasions with all kinds of prayers and requests. With this in mind, be alert and always keep on praying for all the Lord's people." This week, create a prayer journal. Write down the names of people and needs you want to pray for, then choose a few each day to lift up to the Lord.

— Chapter 12 —

A Church on Every Corner

I got my first pair of glasses in fourth grade. By eighth grade I graduated to contacts—rigid gas permeable lenses, otherwise known as optical torture devices. I'd pop them in before school every morning and suffer until dinnertime from shards of plastic stabbing my eyelids. But hey, I was glasses-free, which to an already awkward adolescent was a liberty worth fighting for. Since then I've struggled through every kind of contact lens available to Americans but never found one that didn't feel like sandpaper on my corneas.

Finally, a few months ago, I did something drastic. I got LASIK.

For weeks leading up to the surgery, I was so giddy over the promise of perfect vision that I hadn't stopped to consider the procedure itself. Until the morning of my appointment, when it hit me that a computerized sci-fi laser contraption was about to slice open my eyeballs—my *only* set of eyeballs—and suddenly my stomach twisted into an anxious knot.

That's when I received this text from a friend: "Praying for you and your eyes today!"

I cannot begin to explain how those words touched my heart. Why? Well, because I was freaking out, for one thing, but also? Honestly I forgot I'd even mentioned to this friend that I was having surgery. But she remembered. And she had looked far enough outside of herself to mark down the date, to lift me up in prayer, and to tell me she was doing so. That small yet significant act of kindness—that blessing—gave me the courage I needed to plop my butt in the car and head to the surgeon's office.

Do you know that your prayers matter? They really do. Not because you or I have the power to do anything at all, but because God does. And when His children call on Him in faith, amazing things can happen.

> Therefore I tell you, whatever you ask for in prayer, believe that you have received it, and it will be yours.
>
> Mark 11:24

Following are four stories of how prayer made a difference in the lives of ordinary people like you and me. I dearly hope these will inspire you to believe in the mighty power of prayer, to discover its multiple benefits, and to pray anew with unwavering conviction that our God is able.

Rise Up!

AJ and his wife, Rachel, were like most expectant parents, anxious about the labor and delivery process yet eager to meet their babies—twins, a boy and a girl. They trusted God through every stage of Rachel's pregnancy and wholly believed He would be with them in childbirth as He had been all along. God is faithful. They knew that much.

Yet what they were about to witness would prove beyond a sliver of doubt the enormity of God's power in their lives. And it would undeniably change the way they pray.

146

"Our son, Beckett, was born first, and everything went smoothly," AJ said. "But then an ultrasound of our daughter, Presley, showed something was blocking her delivery, and I was told to leave the room."

AJ paced the hall and prayed fervently with his wife's mom and sister. They heard the overhead speakers call out "Code Pink." Hospital staff whizzed by with carts of equipment, and AJ knew Presley's life was in danger.

"I just kept praying. That was all I knew to do," AJ said. As he waited, he was given a series of updates from Rachel's doctor. Presley had suffered several minutes in the womb deprived of oxygen and blood supply and had lost all the fluids in her body. A nurse performed CPR for twenty minutes until finally the doctor told her to give up and call the time of death. But the nurse refused. AJ was then invited to see his daughter and was told he would have to make some difficult decisions in the coming moments.

When he walked back into the delivery room, he saw his daughter lying on the hospital bed, gray and lifeless. The nurses were continuing to breathe for her. And then, in what he later described as the most charismatic moment of his life, AJ placed his hand on Presley's three-pound body and prayed: "In the name of Jesus, *rise up!*"

And she rose.

"As though lightning struck, her body jolted awake," he said. "She looked at me. She gasped for air. And she lived."

Some doctors called it a medical anomaly. But AJ and his wife know better. To them, Presley's life is nothing short of a bona fide miracle. Even after the Lord brought her back to life, doctors expected Presley to suffer brain damage and cognitive dysfunction. But she did not.

"We received every single thing we prayed for," AJ said. "From not having seizures in those first days, to a good MRI report, to eating on her own, breathing on her own, digesting her food, coming home from the hospital, crawling, standing, walking, developing fine motor skills, talking, playing, laughing—and the list goes on."

Today, the twins are energetic toddlers, best friends, and a living reminder of God's powerful ability to answer our prayers. "Presley is a strong, strong girl," AJ said. "The strength we saw in her in those first days is taking on new forms with each new phase. She lets you know exactly what she wants and won't settle for anything less. She's amazingly fierce but refreshingly gentle."

To God's glory, AJ's family and friends are able to stand on the claim that what they experienced in those first days of Presley's life has proven true: she was healed.

AJ said, "There was a man healed of blindness in John 9 who said, 'Whether [Jesus] is a sinner or not, I don't know. What I do know is this: Once I was blind. Now I can see!' That experience of praying and watching Presley come back ruined me. It took all of the preconceived notions I had of God and myself and tossed them aside.

"I don't know a lot of things," AJ said. "I don't know why God doesn't always do this for families, and especially for children. I don't know why this time, and why us. I don't know what those twenty to thirty minutes looked like in the spiritual world. But what I do know is this: When I put my hand on that little girl, and I spoke the name of Jesus over her, she rose. And now everything is different.

"What we experienced, and what many of our friends and family experienced along with us, is as true today as it was then. Jesus saved. Jesus raised the dead. May we open our eyes to see Him, our ears to hear Him, and our hearts to receive Him."

> I pray that the eyes of your heart may be enlightened in order that you may know the hope to which he has called you, the riches of his glorious inheritance in his holy people, and his incomparably great power for us who believe. That power is the same as the mighty strength he exerted when he raised Christ from the dead and seated him at his right hand in the heavenly realms.
>
> Ephesians 1:18–20

Persevering in Prayer

So what about the times when God doesn't answer "yes"? What about the millions of prayers to which He says "no" or "wait"? What difference does prayer make then?

My friend Bethany would tell you it makes all the difference in the world.

For the past five years, Bethany, her husband, Jeff, and their four children have been waiting to adopt siblings from Haiti. "At first I thought our adoption was about growing our family and being open to God's call on our lives," she explained. "But I've come to realize it's more about learning how to pray and discovering how big prayer is."

International adoption, as many of you know, is a slow and uncertain process. Bethany's family has faced obstacle upon obstacle as they've sifted through mounds of paperwork, endured numerous legal setbacks, and fought a spiritual battle for the hearts of two little girls whom they long to call their own.

These trials might have crushed Bethany. But instead, they bolstered her hope—all thanks to the power of prayer.

"God has grown me so much because of unanswered prayer," she said. "I feel like He has completely changed my prayer life. There have been so many times in this situation when I wanted to do something to make the adoption happen—to move on to the next step of the process or to open a door that was shut. But I know it doesn't work that way. I have to trust God to make it happen."

Bethany has learned to continually give her cares to the Lord—her pleas, anxieties, questions, and tears. "I feel like it's a gift God gives us, this ability to talk to Him," she said. "And that gift, in the long run, is actually more valuable than the answer we've been waiting on."

Trust in the Lord with all your heart and lean not on your own understanding; in all your ways submit to him, and he will make your paths straight.

Proverbs 3:5–6

Praying for her adoption has fueled a fire in Bethany's heart for the Haitian people and all adoptions everywhere. "When you pray for something, you care a lot more about it," she said. "God opens you to it, and then He prompts you to share it with others, who also start praying and caring." Her family is surrounded by a growing circle of friends who pray regularly not just for Bethany's Haitian children but also their entire orphanage and the people of Haiti as a whole.

"I see now that my adoption process, in God's mind, was always so much bigger than my selfish desire in the beginning of having more children. He has used this situation to grow not just me and my family, but also many of my friends, through prayer."

Now when people tell her, "I'm praying for you," Bethany is deeply encouraged. "It reminds me I'm not alone," she said. "Their prayers bless me, *and* they bless two little girls in Haiti who don't have the lives we have. Our girls might come to know Jesus because of these prayers. I feel like it's affecting their lives in ways they don't even know. There's no telling what God is doing behind the scenes!"

Meanwhile, Bethany rests in her abiding hope that the Lord will come through. "I do believe our adoption will happen, I really do. And when it does, we'll realize prayer is not something you do just once. It goes on and on and on."

I remain confident of this: I will see the goodness of the Lord in the land of the living. Wait for the Lord; be strong and take heart and wait for the Lord.

Psalm 27:13–14

When You Have Nothing Else to Give

The beauty of prayer is that it can be done anywhere, anytime, by anyone with a heart tuned to Jesus. Some of the greatest prayer warriors I have known are older women, retired from the workplace, beyond the seasons of caring for their own children or aging parents. More often they are the aging parents, and in their wisest years they remain active servants of Christ by praying—often and ardently—for others. I adore these women. I want to be like them.

So why wait? Even before we reach a more mature stage of life, even before we believe we have the time or the mental space to spare, we can develop a habit of prayer. Start today. Pray for your husband, your children, your friends, your co-workers. Pray while you're washing dishes or driving to work. Pray in the shower, while you're waiting in line for coffee, and in place of channel surfing through bad TV before bed. Then tomorrow, do it again. Make praying for others a part of your lifestyle. And one day, if you reach a stage of life when prayer is all you have left to give, you won't fall apart, because you'll already know praying is the most powerful work a woman can do.

Some of us learn that earlier than others.

Deborah certainly did.

In her early twenties, like many young women—without even realizing it—Deborah defined herself by what she did, her goals, her ministry, and her friends. She was active in her work and social circles. She thrived on being someone others could count on to get the job done.

But then she became ill. Very ill—for several years. She spent a season of her life in a wheelchair, unable to get out of bed. Her youthful vigor gave way to immobility and despair. "I felt so useless," she said. "I'd lost my identity."

Until one day, Deborah's mom spoke truth to her daughter in love. "Honey," her mom told her, "the most powerful thing you can ever do to make yourself useful or to help someone is to pray. And you can do that from your bed."

So she did.

"I found my purpose," Deborah said. "Praying, when I had nothing else to give, changed my perspective. And slowly over those hard years, I learned to define myself by my values, my beliefs, and my status with God—instead of in things I can lose."

The world and its desires pass away, but whoever does the will of God lives forever.

1 John 2:17

Can I Get a Witness?

Remember my friend Alicia from chapter 7? When I introduced you to her, she was buying a mocha for a homeless man. I love her heart for the Lord and her genuine compassion for people of all shapes and sizes. She inspires me to be a better woman.

Alicia lives "across the pond" from my Wisconsin homestead, in a conservative Michigan town with friendly neighborhoods, Christian schools, more than a dozen coffee shops, and a church on every corner. Appearances would profess the community is thriving; therefore, those who *aren't* stand in stark contrast. Like one woman, whom Alicia met at an intersection near a store parking lot.

"She was standing on a dirty snow drift with a sign that said 'Help—Need Work,'" Alicia explained. "I had only two dollars in my wallet, not even enough to buy her lunch, so I turned my head and drove right past."

As she veered toward home, Alicia justified her actions. "I'd only lived in our little town for three weeks, so I didn't even have a friend yet, let alone a personal connection to help the poor woman find work. I wanted to just keep driving back to my safe, comfortable home, but my stomach was lurching with conviction. Finally, I turned my car around and headed back to the corner where the woman stood."

Alicia parked her car nearby, trudged up the dirty snow bank, and handed the woman her measly two dollars. Then she said, "I don't have much money, and I don't know how to help you, but Jesus does. So could I pray with you?"

The woman nodded a tentative *yes*, and together they bowed their heads and prayed right there on the busy street corner. When she opened her eyes, the woman was crying.

A few minutes later, as Alicia walked back to her car, a young woman came rushing toward her. She had witnessed the entire incident from a nearby store window, and with tears running down her cheeks she said, "I've lived here my entire life, and I've never seen anybody do anything like that before."

How can it be? In a town with a church on every corner—a flourishing community where family values are held in high regard and neighbors gladly help each other out—where Christianity is worn like a badge! Is no one willing to pray with a stranger?

Understand I am not talking about praying "like the hypocrites, for they love to pray standing in the synagogues and on the street corners to be seen by others. Truly I tell you, they have received their reward in full" (Matthew 6:5). Alicia did not pray to put on a show. On the contrary, she hesitated. She passed by at first. In her mind, praying with a panhandler was far from pompous; it was awkward and vulnerable. But she did it anyway.

That's what I'm talking about. Praying to look good is hardly our biggest problem in the Christian community these days. The real trouble is we don't pray enough with or in view of others because we're afraid of not looking good. I mean, we don't want to come across as those wacky Jesus nutjobs, right? What will people think of us?! Nah, we'll follow Christ as long as we can blend in with the people who don't. And in so doing, we will deny the world our witness for the One True God.

Not good, sisters. Not good.

Don't become like the people of this world. Instead, change the way you think. Then you will always be able to determine what God really wants—what is good, pleasing, and perfect.

Romans 12:2 GW

For the Love of God—Shine!

As Christ followers, you and I are supposed to be "the light of the world—like a city on a hilltop that cannot be hidden" (Matthew 5:14 NLT). Do you know what happens when a light enters a dark place? It illuminates everything. These days we keep hearing in the media and discussing around the table that our world is getting darker, that there's more evil, more pain, more injustice than ever before. If that's true, then for the love of God, we don't necessarily need to shine brighter—we just need to shine at all.

> If you are generous with the hungry and start giving yourselves to the down-and-out, your lives will begin to glow in the darkness, your shadowed lives will be bathed in sunlight.
>
> Isaiah 58:10 THE MESSAGE

I challenge each and every one of us to stand unashamed, to boldly proclaim our faith to the world around us through blessings. Why not pray with strangers, in public places, on the spur of the moment as the Holy Spirit prompts us? Let's think of our prayers—and our presence, our possessions, our perspective—all the four P's of blessing—like stars. One lonely star has the power to break through the night sky. Imagine, then, billions of stars all at once. All of us, together showering blessings from every corner in every moment, lifting high our intercessions, demonstrating love through actions, training our hearts and minds to *think like God thinks*. Collectively these blessings—this blazing network of constellations—can transform the night, turning darkness to light. Oh, what an amazing world that would be. Amen?

> Those who are wise will shine like the brightness of the heavens, and those who lead many to righteousness, like the stars for ever and ever.
>
> Daniel 12:3

50 Ways to Bless with Your Prayers

1. Be a trustworthy prayer warrior. When someone asks you to pray for them, do it. Be a person they can count on to follow through.
2. Pray whatever comes to mind; don't wait for eloquent words to flow before you decide to bless someone with your prayers.
3. Ask your spouse and children regularly how you can be praying for them.
4. Assign a symbol to represent each key person in your life—for example, chocolate chips for your son who loves cookies, the color purple for your daughter, a motorcycle for your husband who dreams of owning a Harley one day. Then each time you see that symbol, pray for the person associated with it.
5. Pray for your husband's leadership as head of the household—and that the Lord would help you support him.
6. Pray for your children to grow "in wisdom and stature, and in favor with God and man" (Luke 2:52).
7. Pray for people before you text them. Imagine how many prayers this might generate in a day!
8. Every time you brake at a stoplight, pray for someone.
9. Pray for your child's future spouse—and his/her parents.
10. If you have grandchildren, pray specifically for one grandchild each week. Email or text them to ask what's going on in their lives and what they would like prayer for.
11. If you know someone having surgery, pray for the Lord to guide the surgeon's hands.
12. Pray for jail inmates to know the Lord. Pray for their loved ones to endure.
13. Save the Christmas cards you receive from friends and relatives and choose one card/family to pray for each day during mealtime prayers.

14. Pray for your server during the dinner blessing at a restaurant.
15. Pray with and for your children on the drive to school.
16. Pray for your child's teachers—that God would grant them wisdom, kindness, patience, and compassion.
17. Pray for God to protect and strengthen your pastor's family.
18. Ask a friend how you can pray for her.
19. Pray for prebelievers to be saved!
20. Form a prayer group with other parents from your child's school or neighborhood. Pray for each other's children.
21. Organize a prayer group at work. Share weekly prayer requests via email.
22. Pray for the women in your exercise class.
23. Pray for your friends on their birthdays. Thank God for thinking them up!
24. Pray Scripture over your children at bedtime.
25. Set your calendar alerts to remind you of events that matter to your friends, such as a big presentation at work, a scary doctor's appointment, or the anniversary of a loved one's death. Pray for them during those tender times.
26. Write out your prayers for people and mail or email them.
27. While folding clothes or scrubbing pots, pray for the people who use them.
28. Pray for your babies while you rock them.
29. When you invite guests to your home for dinner, pray for them when you say grace.
30. Pray for visitors just before they leave your home—for safe travels and blessings.
31. If you associate certain songs with certain people, pray for them whenever that song comes on the radio.
32. When someone comes to your mind during the day, pray for them—then let them know you did. Often God prompts us to intercede for another before we know why.

33. When you hear an ambulance, fire truck, or police siren, pray for the people involved—and thank God for your blessings.
34. Pray for your local police officers.
35. Pray for the sanitation workers on garbage day.
36. Pray for your friends to know how beautiful they are in Christ.
37. When you tell someone you'll pray for their family member, be sure to ask the person's name and write it down. Praying for people by name makes it a more personal gesture.
38. If you see someone crying during a church service, lift them up to the Lord.
39. Each day, choose one person or family who does not know the Lord and pray for their salvation.
40. Pray for our nation's leaders.
41. Pray for each of your neighbors as you drive or walk down your street.
42. Keep a ring of index cards in your car, with a prayer prompt written on each one. Flip through these when you're waiting to pick up kids or are stuck in traffic.
43. Keep a prayer journal for thirty days for someone in particular and present it to that person afterward as tangible evidence of your prayers.
44. Pray through your church bulletin—for your church leaders, outreach, ministries, and events.
45. Write prayers on note cards "for the recipient" and leave them in hotel room Bibles or library books.
46. Ask your kids to pray something specific for you, then tell them you're praying for them, too. This will help teach them about the power of blessing people with prayer.
47. "Adopt" a missionary family by praying for them regularly.
48. Pray for the janitorial staff at school or work.
49. Pray for your boss to lead well and with a servant's heart.
50. Keep a prayer journal for each of your children and present it to them as a gift on their wedding day.

——— Let's Dig Deeper ———

1. The stories in this chapter illustrate four key truths about prayer:
   1. Prayer produces results (AJ's baby girl).
   2. Prayer is a catalyst for spiritual growth (Bethany's adoption process).
   3. Prayer is an act of service (Deborah's inability to serve except for prayer).
   4. Prayer is a witness for Christ (Alicia's prayer with the woman on the street).

   Which of these four truths/stories impacted you most? Did they reveal any ideas about prayer and its role in your life that you had not considered before?

2. Think of a time when you prayed for something and God answered. How did this impact your faith in prayer?

3. Do you believe in miracles? Remember, God is unchanging (Malachi 3:6; James 1:17; Hebrews 13:8). The same God who performed miracles in biblical times is watching over us today. See Genesis 21:2; Exodus 16:21; Jonah 2:10; Daniel 6:16–23; Matthew 1:18; Matthew 14:25–27; and John 11:38–44. What do these passages tell you about God's power?

4. Have you ever been in a situation of waiting on God? How did God use that time to grow you?

5. Think of someone you know who is an avid prayer warrior. What do you admire about that person? What can you learn from her/him?

6. In your own words, explain why prayer is action.

158

7. Have you been in a situation similar to Alicia's? How did you respond? Why might prayer have been a bigger gift than Alicia's two dollars?

8. What keeps you from shining the light of Christ? How have these past several chapters impacted your desire to serve God by blessing others?

Love in Motion

This week, whenever you encounter someone in need of prayer, don't just tell them "I'll pray for you." Actually stop what you're doing and pray in the moment. Discover how this impacts your spiritual growth and relationships.

— Chapter 13 —

Why? Because God Says So

So far we've discussed what a blessing is and how to grant one. We've explored our inherent selfishness and flawed perspectives, and we've equipped our toolbox with ample insight, encouragement, and practical tips to begin shifting our hearts, souls, minds, and strength toward God's will—to achieve the goal of loving other people well.

But one huge question remains.

Why?

Why in heaven's name should we love people? Why bless them? Why bother? What's the whole big fat fuzzy point?

I'm so glad you asked.

In this chapter and the next, we're going to address that question with two loud and clear answers from Scripture:

1. Because God says so.
2. Because it benefits you.

In that order.

Because God Says So

When I was a child, my mom would tell me to pick up my toys. My juvenile reasoning usually had some better plan in mind—such as continuing to play with the toys or else leave them for *her* to pick up—so I'd ask the dead-end question: *Why?*

And of course my mom, being a good and classic parent, would respond with those words we all loathe hearing. You know 'em, I know 'em, we swore we'd never say them to our own children, but we do: *Because I said so.*

Grrrr! I detest that answer! Give me an explanation, woman! Let's debate our motives and our consequences here. But no. Mom was the authority. I was just the kid. Therefore, I had no choice but to take it on blind faith that my mother had her reasons for commanding a toy pickup at that very moment in time and space—and my job was to do it.

God is our ultimate authority. He is our heavenly Father. He knows what's best for us when we haven't got a clue. We owe Him our deepest, fullest respect and obedience. And it's true that sometimes we won't know why He tells us to take a certain action, make a certain choice, or endure a certain hardship. We just need to trust it's for our own good.

Yet here's the really cool thing about God. In a general sense, He does explain. He does give us good reasons for demonstrating love, joy, peace, patience, kindness, goodness, faithfulness, gentleness, and self-control. Those traits are straight-up fruit of the Spirit (Galatians 5:22–23), which means, if you're a Jesus follower, they're already in you. Therefore, God simply expects you to *be who you really are.*

Let's examine a series of God's commands and truths from Scripture, and discover how they point us to generous love.

Love God and Others

Hearing that Jesus had silenced the Sadducees, the Pharisees got together. One of them, an expert in the law, tested him with this question: "Teacher, which is the greatest commandment in the Law?" Jesus replied: "'Love the Lord your God with all your heart and with all your soul and with all your mind.' This is the first and greatest commandment. And the second is like it: 'Love your neighbor as yourself.' All the Law and the Prophets hang on these two commandments."

Matthew 22:34–40

Don't you find it interesting that when Jesus was asked to name the top commandment, He named not one but two? This ought to tell us that loving God is inseparable from loving people. Loving God comes first, because God *is* love (1 John 4:8). He equips us to love. He is worthy of our deepest love and adoration not just because of what He does for us but more so because of who He is—our all-knowing, all-loving, ever-faithful, almighty Father, the source of all blessings. Our love for others is then a natural outpouring of our love for God. "*We love because he first loved us*" (1 John 4:19).

In fact, the Bible says loving people is actually how we prove our love for God. Wow.

By this everyone will know that you are my disciples, if you love one another.

John 13:35

So let me ask a question. Why do so many of us stink at it?

Loving people is hard. Our selfishness battles our desire to do what's right, or worse, it blinds us to the opportunity in the first place. Even the apostle Paul, the greatest evangelist in history, struggled with this inner war.

I want to do what is good, but I don't. I don't want to do what is wrong, but I do it anyway. But if I do what I don't want to do, I am not really the one doing wrong; it is sin living in me that does it.

Romans 7:19–20 NLT

Sin is definitely a major obstacle to obeying God's commands. But for the believer, it goes even deeper than that. Could it be that the reason we don't love others well is because we're not totally convinced of God's love for us?

No, no, no, you say. I'm a Christian; I accepted Christ ages ago. I know He's crazy about me! That's Jesus Saves 101!

Huh. Okay. Are you truly living like you believe that?

Think about it. It's really not that amazing that we would love Jesus. I mean, He's pretty fantastic. What's far more amazing is that He would love *us*. Compared to His perfection, His holiness, His majesty, we are pitifully flawed and ugly.

> When I consider your heavens, the work of your fingers, the moon and the stars, which you have set in place, what is mankind that you are mindful of them, human beings that you care for them?
>
> Psalm 8:3–4

And yet, God does love us. He doesn't have to; He *wants to*! It's the same way we humans bring home a wrinkled, blotchy, mewling newborn baby who has nothing to give but midnight screams and runny diapers—yet moms, dads, and grandparents cherish that tiny creature as though there's nothing more beautiful in all the world. Because they're our children.

When we begin to understand just how magnificent and irrational God's love for us really is, we are wrecked—in a good way. We can finally shed our selfish skin and be set free to love others, because we are face-on-the-ground grateful to God for loving us first.

> For I am convinced that neither death nor life, neither angels nor demons, neither the present nor the future, nor any powers, neither height nor depth, nor anything else in all creation, will be able to separate us from the love of God that is in Christ Jesus our Lord.
>
> Romans 8:38–39

That's why it's vital to pursue God above all other things. Spending time with Jesus, studying God's Word, hearing His voice, enjoying His company, getting to know Him more and more—these will reveal to us the enormity of His love and mercy. They will win us over to His trust. And only then can we truly bless others, simply because we're giving them what we already possess: crazy, beautiful, life-saving love.

Love Is an Obligation We Owe to Others

> Owe nothing to anyone—except for your obligation to love one another. If you love your neighbor, you will fulfill the requirements of God's law.
>
> Romans 13:8 NLT

The Bible calls love a debt we owe to others. We are forever indebted to Jesus for dying on the cross for us, yet because our salvation is a free gift (Ephesians 2:8–9), God doesn't command us to repay Him directly. He wants us to pay out our dues to other people, our neighbors. Understand this includes people within the church family and beyond it—people we enjoy or dislike or don't know at all. Loving them is an act of loving God. It fulfills the debt we cannot pay.

Throughout Scripture God makes it clear that we are not supposed to be burdened by impossible debts; however, love is an exception. Love is the obligation that can never be fully satisfied. We must constantly pay it out.

> Therefore if you have any encouragement from being united with Christ, if any comfort from his love, if any common sharing in the Spirit, if any tenderness and compassion, then make my joy complete by being like-minded, having the same love, being one in spirit and of one mind.
>
> Philippians 2:1–2

Love Gives Our Actions Worth

If I speak in the tongues of men or of angels, but do not have love, I am only a resounding gong or a clanging cymbal. If I have the gift of prophecy and can fathom all mysteries and all knowledge, and if I have a faith that can move mountains, but do not have love, I am nothing. If I give all I possess to the poor and give over my body to hardship that I may boast, but do not have love, I gain nothing.

1 Corinthians 13:1–3

There is a difference between nice and kind. Nice is a mood; it leads to exterior gestures. Kind is a virtue; it generates blessings that flow from deep within. Exterior gestures can be done in our own strength. Blessings require the love and strength of God. And guess what—we don't get credit for what we've done if it's not rooted in love.

The Bible says I can have the incredible ability to speak angel talk (can you imagine?!), possess all knowledge of all subjects in the world, even give up every single little thing I own—but if I do it without love, I'm just an inflated ego. God counts it as nothing.

He would rather see me give a penny from a heart of love than a million dollars from a selfish motive. The love behind the action matters that much.

A person may think their own ways are right, but the Lord weighs the heart.

Proverbs 21:2

Love Is Humble

Therefore, as God's chosen people, holy and dearly loved, clothe yourselves with compassion, kindness, humility, gentleness and patience.

Colossians 3:12

Here's a caution flag in the generous love process: Don't expect anybody to praise you for your selflessness. It defeats the whole purpose.

I know it's only human nature to want some recognition for your good deeds. A simple "thank you" or some homemade pie, maybe—doesn't even have to be the whole pie, just give me a slice, right? Cherry, apple, pumpkin, whatever. I'm not picky.

But if living "others first" is meant to display the love of Christ, then we cannot demand kudos. Our actions must be rooted in humility. Why?

Because that's who Christ is.

In your relationships with one another, have the same mindset as Christ Jesus: Who, being in very nature God, did not consider equality with God something to be used to his own advantage; rather, he made himself nothing by taking the very nature of a servant, being made in human likeness. And being found in appearance as a man, he humbled himself by becoming obedient to death—even death on a cross! Therefore God exalted him to the highest place and gave him the name that is above every name, that at the name of Jesus every knee should bow, in heaven and on earth and under the earth, and every tongue acknowledge that Jesus Christ is Lord, to the glory of God the Father.

Philippians 2:5–11

Humility is what will allow us to bless freely, even when it's hard. It will enable us to see others as worthy of our love, even when they're scary or unattractive or odd. And—don't you just love the irony of God?—only humility will bring the greatest rewards in the end.

For those who exalt themselves will be humbled, and those who humble themselves will be exalted.

Matthew 23:12

Maintain Gratitude and Reverence

Work hard to show the results of your salvation, obeying God with deep reverence and fear.

Philippians 2:12 NLT

Now, let's consider the reverse question. Why *wouldn't* we bless someone? Well, I can think of a few reasons.

- We don't want to.
- We don't like them.
- We don't think they deserve it.
- We don't agree with the concept.
- We're too busy.
- We don't recognize the need.

All of these excuses point to one culprit: We have lost respect for God.

Romans 1:20 says, "For since the creation of the world God's invisible qualities—his eternal power and divine nature—have been clearly seen, being understood from what has been made, so that people are without excuse." God's divine nature is visible to us. It's everywhere we look! It's in the sunrise, the oak trees, the snowflakes, and the sandy beach. All of creation screams *Awesome Creator*, yet we cease to recognize Him—because it's all too familiar.

I drive the same route to and from my daughters' school day after day after day. I could probably make it at least halfway with my eyes closed (although I won't—come on now—stoplights, hello). The streets are so familiar to me, I rarely look at the signs anymore or notice the color of the houses lining the road. I don't have to. I already know.

The same thing happens when we stare God's creation in the face day after day after day. It becomes too familiar. Then we start thinking we don't need to pay attention to what He says—loving people, showing kindness, seeing others the way God sees them—because there's no more wonder in the journey. There's no more awe. We've squandered our reverence for who God is and what He has done.

And sadly, we lose our desire to follow.

Dear friends, since God so loved us, we also ought to love one
another.

1 John 4:11

The solution is simple. We need a fresh respect for Jesus. We
need to compare our smallness to His greatness. Then we'll have
a fresh respect for doing what He says.

And how do we get a fresh respect for Jesus? Open your eyes.
Look around. Rediscover the beauty in your surroundings, in nature, in music, in the sound of your child's laugh. Meditate on the
great lengths to which He sacrificed himself for your salvation.
Try counting the stars, for heaven's sake! That alone will blow
your mind!

Rekindle your reverence for God, and you will be inspired once
again to follow Him—and to share His love with others.

Restore to me the joy of your salvation and grant me a willing spirit,
to sustain me.

Psalm 51:12

Do the One-Anothers

Don't just pretend to love others. Really love them. Hate what is
wrong. Hold tightly to what is good. Love each other with genuine
affection, and take delight in honoring each other.

Romans 12:9–10 NLT

Some of my favorite verses in the Bible are the "one-anothers."
These are the verses that describe how we ought to treat other
people. They confirm the fact that God created us to be in community with each other and to care about people beyond ourselves.
You've read some of them already so far in this book; I'll remind
you of some again before we're done. But for now, it seems only
fitting to wrap up our chapter "Because God Says So" with His

instructions for *how*. Read them. Memorize them. Tape them to your bathroom mirrors and save them in your phone. Make these words a part of your heart. Then "do not merely listen to the word and so deceive yourselves. Do what it says" (James 1:22).

Love one another.

"A new command I give you: Love one another. As I have loved you, so you must love one another" (John 13:34).

"Dear friends, since God so loved us, we also ought to love one another" (1 John 4:11).

"Above all, love each other deeply, because love covers over a multitude of sins" (1 Peter 4:8).

Pray for one another.

"Therefore confess your sins to each other and pray for each other so that you may be healed. The prayer of a righteous man is powerful and effective" (James 5:16).

"And pray in the Spirit on all occasions with all kinds of prayers and requests. With this in mind, be alert and always keep on praying for all the Lord's people" (Ephesians 6:18).

Encourage one another.

"Therefore encourage one another and build each other up, just as in fact you are doing" (1 Thessalonians 5:11).

"But encourage one another daily, as long as it is called 'Today,' so that none of you may be hardened by sin's deceitfulness" (Hebrews 3:13).

"And let us consider how we may spur one another on toward love and good deeds. Let us not give up meeting together, as some are in the habit of doing, but let us encourage one another— and all the more as you see the Day approaching" (Hebrews 10:24–25).

Hold one another accountable.

"Brothers and sisters, if someone is caught in a sin, you who live by the Spirit should restore that person gently" (Galatians 6:1).

"Instead, speaking the truth in love, we will in all things grow up into him who is the Head, that is, Christ" (Ephesians 4:15).

Carry one another's burdens.

"Carry each other's burdens, and in this way you will fulfill the law of Christ" (Galatians 6:2).

Teach one another.

"Let the message of Christ dwell among you richly as you teach and admonish one another with all wisdom through psalms, hymns, and songs from the Spirit, singing to God with gratitude in your hearts" (Colossians 3:16).

"Likewise, teach the older women to be reverent in the way they live, not to be slanderers or addicted to much wine, but to teach what is good. Then they can train the younger women to love their husbands and children, to be self-controlled and pure, to be busy at home, to be kind, and to be subject to their husbands, so that no one will malign the word of God" (Titus 2:3–5).

Serve one another.

"Now that I, your Lord and Teacher, have washed your feet, you also should wash one another's feet" (John 13:14).

"You, my brothers and sisters, were called to be free. But do not use your freedom to indulge the flesh; rather, serve one another humbly in love" (Galatians 5:13).

───── **Let's Dig Deeper** ─────

1. Read 1 John 4:7–21. Where does love come from? What makes it possible? According to this passage, what one characteristic marks a person as belonging to God? What does this tell you about the importance of generous love?

2. John 13:35 says a person is identified as a Jesus follower not according to how she loves God, but rather how she loves other people. How is loving others a demonstration of our love for God?

3. Rate the degree to which you believe the following statements. (1=I don't believe this at all; 5=There's not a doubt in my mind.)

   God loves me. .... 1 ..2 ..3 ..4 ..5

   Jesus died for me (yes, me!). .... 1 ..2 ..3 ..4 ..5

   Nothing I do can make God love me less. .... 1 ..2 ..3 ..4 ..5

   Nothing I do can make God love me more. 1 ..2 ..3 ..4 ..5

   God has forgiven all the bad stuff I've done. 1 ..2 ..3 ..4 ..5

   If you are unsure of how to answer these questions, revisit our discussion in chapter 2, "Jesus: The Life-Changer." Share your doubts with a godly friend or your Bible study leader.

4. Look again at Romans 13:8. How does blessing others fulfill our obligation to love one another?

5. What is the difference between *nice* and *kind*? How are Christians equipped with the unique ability to demonstrate real kindness? (Hint: see Galatians 5:22–23.)

6. Read Matthew 6:2. Why is humility an important aspect of blessing others? How are ulterior motives and pride counterproductive to the process of living "others first"?

7. What reasons do you harbor for *not* blessing others (or someone in particular)? What does the Bible say about that? See 1 John 4:11–12 and 4:20–21.

8. Romans 12:10 (NLT) tells us, "Love each other with genuine affection, and take delight in honoring each other." Do you take delight in honoring other people? Why or why not?

Love in Motion

This week focus on rekindling your reverence for God. Be intentional about looking for God's beauty in nature, art, science, food, etc. Open your heart to detect Him working in your daily life. Pray for restored awe and joy over the things of the Lord. Memorize Psalm 51:12 and call those words out to your heavenly Father.

— Chapter 14 —

And Because
It Benefits You, Too

My daughters are saving for a puppy. That's what they tell us, anyway. Whether or not Daddy and I have decided we're ready to adopt a furry friend is immaterial at this point; they are determined that if they can afford it, they will have it. We admire their tenacity.

So on a regular basis, they'll ask if I have any chores for them to do. *Sure*, I'll nod, *how sweet of you to ask! You can fold laundry, you can dust, you can empty the dishwasher. Mom's got lots of chores!*

To which they reply: *How much are you going to pay me?*

Ah. Naturally. It's the give-and-take philosophy of modern culture. If I do this, you'll do that. If I give this, you'll give that. If I work hard, you will pay me a dollar. If I scrub the bathtub, you'll eventually let me get a puppy.

To some degree this concept is actually quite biblical. Throughout Scripture God tells His people, *If you obey me, I will reward you.* The Israelites heard it again and again and again—and they still disobeyed (again and again and again). Some things never change.

Yet understand this: The reward is not really the goal. It's just a perk.

Why should we love others? Because God tells us to, period, exclamation point, end of story. The second reason—because it benefits us—is not meant to be a primary motive. True blessings are not granted with the intent of getting something in return. The giving is a reward in itself, as Jesus tells us, "It is more blessed to give than to receive" (Acts 20:35). And still, because God is such a loving Father, He *does* reward us for a job well done. It's a fringe benefit of trusting Him.

Obedience Brings Blessing

The Bible is packed with promises that we will be blessed if we do what God says. It's part of God's system. Just look at all the ways He expresses this truth throughout Scripture (emphasis added).

Anyone who listens to the word but does not do what it says is like someone who looks at his face in a mirror and, after looking at himself, goes away and immediately forgets what he looks like. But whoever looks intently into the perfect law that gives freedom, and continues in it—not forgetting what they have heard, but doing it—*they will be blessed in what they do* (James 1:23–25).

I will surely bless you and make your descendants as numerous as the stars in the sky and as the sand on the seashore. Your descendants will take possession of the cities of their enemies, and through your offspring all nations on earth will be blessed, *because you have obeyed me* (Genesis 22:17–18).

Those who are kind benefit themselves, but the cruel bring ruin on themselves (Proverbs 11:17).

The generous will themselves be blessed, for they share their food with the poor (Proverbs 22:9).

Give, and it will be given to you. A good measure, pressed down, shaken together and running over, will be poured into your lap. For with the measure you use, it will be measured to you (Luke 6:38).

"Truly I tell you," Jesus said to them, "no one who has left home or wife or brothers or sisters or parents or children for the sake of the kingdom of God will fail to *receive many times as much* in this age, and in the age to come eternal life" (Luke 18:29–30).

Remember this: Whoever sows sparingly will also reap sparingly, and whoever sows generously will also reap generously (2 Corinthians 9:6).

Whoever is kind to the poor lends to the Lord, and *he will reward them* for what they have done (Proverbs 19:17).

"Bring the whole tithe into the storehouse, that there may be food in my house. Test me in this," says the Lord Almighty, "and see if I will not throw open the floodgates of heaven and *pour out so much blessing* that there will not be room enough to store it" (Malachi 3:10).

Those who live only to satisfy their own sinful nature will harvest decay and death from that sinful nature. But those who live to please the Spirit will harvest everlasting life from the Spirit. So *let's not get tired of doing what is good. At just the right time we will reap a harvest of blessing if we don't give up.* Therefore, whenever we have the opportunity, we should do good to everyone—especially to those in the family of faith (Galatians 6:8–10 NLT).

Do you see? The Bible is explicit on this topic. Generous love— obeying the "one-anothers" and showing love in action as God commands us to do—*will be rewarded.* That central truth, while it ought not be our primary reason for loving others, is certainly a pretty awesome benefit of living for Christ. It should spur our gratitude and energize our hearts, so we do "not get tired of doing what is good."

What Are the Rewards?

I know, I know. Some of you are throwing this book at the wall right now. Thank you for picking it back up off the floor, my broken-hearted sister. I get it. I have the same questions. *Where's my reward, right? Why haven't I seen it yet?*

Ah. God's economy is so different from ours. His reward system may not be at all what we expect. Often we long for recognition, comfort, restored relationships, you name it.

I've done what you told me to do, Lord! Now give me my marriage back! Give me healing! Give me financial rescue, salvation for my loved ones, the dream job I've been coveting forever! For crying out loud, Jesus, just give me a nap or a hot shower!

We want our rewards to come in the shape of that thing we've been waiting on, praying for, crying over. But God doesn't always grant us those desires. Why? Because He never fails to give us the better gift. And more than anything else, our heavenly Father knows we need more of Him.

That is the greatest reward—whether we realize it or not.

> The same Lord is Lord of all and richly blesses all who call on him, for, "Everyone who calls on the name of the Lord will be saved."
>
> Romans 10:12–13

Getting More of God

So what does that mean, anyway—getting "more of God"? Seems like a bizarre concept, right? But it's real. When we receive more of God, we starting thinking the way He thinks and wanting more of what He wants. He infuses us with deeper peace, firmer trust, and fuller joy. These are not the tangible, measurable rewards we often long for—but they're so much better.

There's a sobering account in the Old Testament that illustrates this concept. In Genesis chapter 13, we find an account of Abraham and his nephew Lot. Both men were wealthy and successful, which in those days meant they possessed acres of herds, flocks, and tents, plus an army of servants required to care for them all. Eventually the land in which God had placed the two men couldn't contain their combined bounty, so they parted ways.

Abraham allowed Lot to choose first, and Lot went east to pitch his tents near Sodom, a city known for its wickedness. Abraham went the opposite direction to a great forest, where God blessed him with provision of every kind.

Later in chapter 18, Abraham is visited by three angels. Many theologians believe the third angel was Jesus, who appears in certain Old Testament scenes as "the angel of God." Can you imagine? Three angels show up for dinner, and one of them is Jesus Christ himself! What an amazing gift, to be in the direct presence of the Holy One.

Lot, however, had put himself in a precarious situation, living among the Sodomites who "were sinning greatly against the Lord" (Genesis 13:13). Rather than living in faith as Abraham had done, Lot immersed himself in the surrounding irreverent culture. He still belonged to God, but his convictions wavered. So when God sent angels to visit Lot in chapter 19, He sent only two. Jesus was not among them.

What does this tell us? Obedience—doing what God tells us to do, living a life that seeks to please Him—is rewarded. *With more of God.*

That Doesn't Mean It's Going to Be Easy

A friend of mine shared a teaching recently about Psalm 121 that spoke to some personal struggles she was going through at the time. "In a year where God has been systematically removing many of the things in my life that I hold dear—health, friendships, security, pride, all my false gods—I have been more blessed and encouraged by the Word than ever before," she said. "For me, having 'more Jesus' is an invisible hope that makes me believe—even in the depths of despair—I'm not alone."

> I lift up my eyes to the mountains—where does my help come from? My help comes from the Lord, the Maker of heaven and earth. He will not let your foot slip—he who watches over you will not slumber; indeed, he who watches over Israel will neither slumber nor sleep. The Lord watches over you—the Lord is your shade at your right hand; the sun will not harm you by day, nor the moon by night. The Lord will keep you from all harm—he will watch over your life; the Lord will watch over your coming and going both now and forevermore.

> Psalm 121

This particular psalm was likely written when the psalmist was making his way to Jerusalem to worship at a pilgrimage feast. This was no trip to the beach. The hills surrounding God's Holy City were notorious for bandits, wild animals, dangerous land features, and brutal weather, not to mention pagan shrines, which at that time were active strongholds for demonic oppression. Sound fun? No way.

To get to his destination—the place of worship, the place where he knew he would be blessed by the presence of God—the traveler had to climb through all these difficulties. Nowhere in the psalm does it say God beamed the pilgrim up to Jerusalem just because he was seeking Him. But it does say the Lord was "a shade at His right hand" and the Lord "watched over his coming and going both now and forevermore." God walked *with him* through the challenges, and He does the same for us. He protects us and guides us when we, like the pilgrim, are longing for more of Him.

As my friend said, "Sometimes we walk through the valley of the shadow of death in our attempt to gain more Jesus. It is in these times that He refines us through testing and trial. He adds bulk to our spiritual muscle through the pain and toil of the journey.

We may not see our growth or the solutions we desire, but He is at work minimizing us so He can maximize himself."

Generous Loving Lifts Your Spirits

We've explored how God can grow us closer to Him as a reward for obedience in times of suffering. Ironically, He can also use our suffering to console us—when we focus on something beyond our heartache.

Keri's son, Mason, has muscular dystrophy. At only seven years old, he has already endured several invasive surgeries and recently underwent a major procedure on his spine. No matter how many times they've been through it, preparing for surgery is a stressful experience for Keri and her family. No mom wants to see her child in pain.

But rather than dwelling on her fears, Keri decided to pour her energy into helping someone else. Just weeks before the surgery, her family held a shoe drive to benefit Soles for Jesus, a ministry that delivers shoes to children in developing countries so they can attend school.

"Mason can't run. He's not a kid that wears out shoes," Keri said. "There was something really cool in the idea that while he uses shoes and certainly needs them, we don't wear them out, we just outgrow them. So we were in a perfect position to give up our gently used shoes to kids whose lives will be changed because of a simple pair of sneakers."

Keri announced her shoe drive on Facebook and was stunned by the response. Neighbors, friends, co-workers, and people from Mason's school community dropped off pair after pair of shoes on Keri's doorstep. Her husband's employer supported the shoe drive by offering raffle tickets to anyone who donated. The day before surgery, Keri's family delivered more than two hundred pairs of shoes to Soles for Jesus—and they've continued collecting shoes ever since.

"When you're going through something stressful, I forget that other people have their own problems," Keri said. "Our stress was not an excuse. We always say we're not going to be victims of this disease; we're going to live in victory. The shoe drive was one of the ways we could do that. It helped us all focus on how we're still in a position of blessing."

In the end, Keri said, although the shoe drive was about blessing other people, she and her family were blessed more. "People always want to help you when you're going through a crisis," she said. "The shoe effort gave them something so simple and tangible that they could do, to feel like they were reaching out to serve us, but really they were also serving someone else in the process. It was a two-for-one! The whole experience really lifted our spirits and helped us to focus outward instead of inward on our pain and anxiety."

A generous person will prosper; whoever refreshes others will be refreshed.

Proverbs 11:25

Blessing Begets More Blessing

The benefits of obeying God's commands to love do not stop with us personally. With each blessing, the yield proliferates and spreads throughout God's kingdom whenever one blessing sparks another, which sparks another, which sparks another and another and another ad infinitum. This may not happen with every act of generosity we deliver, especially when our blessings land on hardened hearts. We'll talk more about that in the next chapter. But for now, understand that single small blessings *can* mushroom. And the more we take a chance at blessing others, the greater the probability that one of them is going to stick—and multiply.

Like this one.

Alba and her husband, Matt, were called to be missionaries at the same time Alba learned she was pregnant with their first child.

This ministry opportunity meant moving far away from family and accepting a huge cut in income.

"I knew that God was calling us to step out in faith, but I was worried about my baby," Alba said. "I didn't mind living on very little for myself, but having a baby put everything in a different perspective." She struggled with wanting to provide for her daughter the way she imagined she could, had they not been offered the new job.

"One thing I was really worried about for some reason was clothing for her," Alba said. "I kept praying for God to speak to me about this and calm my heart."

Then one day as she was reading her Bible, the hymn "His Eye Is on the Sparrow" came on the radio. It brought to Alba's mind a passage from the book of Matthew where Jesus says,

> "Look at the birds of the air; they do not sow or reap or store away in barns, and yet your heavenly Father feeds them. Are you not much more valuable than they? . . . And why do you worry about clothes? See how the flowers of the field grow. They do not labor or spin. Yet I tell you that not even Solomon in all his splendor was dressed like one of these. If that is how God clothes the grass of the field, which is here today and tomorrow is thrown into the fire, will he not much more clothe you—you of little faith?"
>
> Matthew 6:26, 28–30

"From there I felt that God was telling me He was going to provide for us, especially in the clothing category," Alba said.

Fast forward several months; Alba and Matt made the big move and welcomed their beautiful baby girl, Elisabeth. They had a few outfits in newborn and three-month sizes but not much more. Still, Alba kept reminding herself that God had promised to provide.

Then, strolling through the church hallway one day, a woman stopped to introduce herself to Alba. It turned out she had a daughter born almost exactly a year before Elisabeth. The woman, Stephanie, asked Alba if she would like to have any of her daughter's clothes, and of course Alba jumped at the chance. "A few days later," Alba said, "Stephanie showed up at my door with twenty-two boxes of baby clothes. I couldn't believe my eyes!"

Most of the outfits had been obtained as gifts and were still in perfect condition. There were so many, neither Stephanie's daughter nor Alba's could possibly wear them all. Yet Alba graciously accepted the plenitude.

At the same time, Alba's parents began taking several mission trips to Cuba. They noticed the Cubans had a huge need for—wouldn't you know it—baby clothes. Alba was able to fill four suitcases from the overflow of God's provision, which her parents distributed to women in need.

Today, Alba's daughter is a toddler, and Stephanie keeps on passing down clothing, which Alba continues sharing with her fellow moms in Cuba.

Isn't it amazing? There's just no telling how God will use our small steps of faith and obedience to bless us and, through us, other people, as well—even those we may never meet and in ways we may never fully see.

Now to him who is able to do immeasurably more than all we ask or imagine, according to his power that is at work within us, to him be glory in the church and in Christ Jesus throughout all generations, for ever and ever! Amen.

Ephesians 3:20–21

———— **Let's Dig Deeper** ————

1. James 1:25 says, "But whoever looks intently into the perfect law that gives freedom, and continues in it—not forgetting what they have heard, but doing it—they will be blessed in what they do." How does obeying God's "perfect law" give us freedom? See 2 Corinthians 3:17; John 8:36; Acts 13:38–39; and Romans 6:22.

2. Read Proverbs 11:17. How do those who are kind benefit themselves?

3. See Luke 6:38 and 2 Corinthians 9:6. Both of these verses refer to the principle of sowing and reaping. How does this affect the way you look at blessing others?

4. Read Matthew 7:9–11. How can our idea of a good gift be quite different from God's? How can we be sure that whatever God gives us is somehow in our best interest? See Romans 8:28–32 for insight.

5. What does it mean to receive "more of God"? How do we do this?

6. Read John 15:2. Have you ever experienced a season of pruning? According to this verse, why might God allow us to go through struggles or loss? How can this be for our benefit?

7. Proverbs 11:25 says "whoever refreshes others will be refreshed." Think of a time when it blessed you to bless someone else. What was your experience?

8. In your own words, why is it more blessed to give than to receive (Acts 20:35)?

Love in Motion

Start keeping a journal of all the ways you see God blessing you for your obedience. In seasons of struggle, remember that God's blessings may not always look the way you expect, but that doesn't mean He's not still working in your life.

— Chapter 15 —

When Blessing Is Hard

At Christmastime, Jill took her children shopping to buy gifts for their dad. Like so many other families, they wandered through aisles of neckties, power tools, sporting goods, and coffee mugs until they settled on just the right Christmas presents for the guy who, in his children's eyes, can do no wrong.

Jill knew otherwise.

Through fourteen years of marriage, her husband had been unfaithful. She forgave, they sought counseling, she forgave some more. Jill knew God commanded her to love her husband even through his flaws, and she worked hard every day at putting him first, supporting his career, expecting nothing in return, and instilling those same selfless values in their children. Yet her husband held to his own greed and deceit, until finally their marriage ended in divorce.

Two years later, the heartbreak still surfaces in tears.

"I find solace in knowing I did what was asked of me," Jill said. "In the beginning I served and blessed my husband because I thought it was expected of me in marriage, but as time went on and there was no reciprocity, I did it more because it was obedience to the Lord."

Now, raising her three children as a single mom, Jill fights an inner battle. "My sin nature doesn't want to do anything kind for someone who has treated me so badly," she explained. "But I want to be a vessel for my kids; I don't want my junk to rub off on them. I have to pray all the time and ask God to help me, to give me strength to obey Him."

You think Jill has a right to be ugly? That her ex-husband doesn't deserve such mercy after everything he did? That's what the world shouts in her face every day. But God says something different.

> Do not repay evil with evil or insult with insult. On the contrary, repay evil with blessing, because to this you were called so that you may inherit a blessing.
>
> 1 Peter 3:9

"Everything in me wants to be bitter and resentful and hurt, but obeying is breaking that instinct," Jill said. "As a follower of Christ I live for something more than myself and my desires and my feelings. Resentment eats you from the inside out. It prevents you from healing. There is no freedom in that. But there is freedom in choosing to encourage my kids to keep loving and blessing their dad. And hopefully one day they will understand and appreciate how I handled this very difficult situation—for their benefit, and for God's glory."

There's no way around it. Sometimes blessing others is downright hard. It feels painful, foolish, even futile. Yet God still calls us to do it.

How? How can we possibly bless people who wound us, who grate on our nerves, or wish us ill and offer no chance of blessing us back?

We can't. That's why we need God—because *He* can.

> But love your enemies, do good to them, and lend to them without expecting to get anything back. Then your reward will be great, and

you will be children of the Most High, because he is kind to the ungrateful and wicked. Be merciful, just as your Father is merciful.

Luke 6:35–36

If God is our model, then we have no excuse. He is kind to the ungrateful and wicked; therefore, we must also be kind—to people who, in our fleshly opinion, deserve to be buried alive in a pit of poisonous snakes. No! God says love them! Do good to them! And— stab me now, Jesus—*don't expect anything in return!* Whaaaat??? How is that possible?

With God.

But he said to me, "My grace is sufficient for you, for my power is made perfect in weakness." Therefore I will boast all the more gladly about my weaknesses, so that Christ's power may rest on me. That is why, for Christ's sake, I delight in weaknesses, in insults, in hardships, in persecutions, in difficulties. For when I am weak, then I am strong.

2 Corinthians 12:9–10

Sacrifice Is Part of Our Calling

Wouldn't it be nice if living for Jesus meant we never had any problems? We'd never get hurt, never encounter nasty people, never have to do anything we didn't want to do—and, as a result, we'd never grow.

In the Old Testament, God commands, "Do not seek revenge or bear a grudge against anyone among your people, but love your neighbor as yourself" (Leviticus 19:18). When Jesus comes on the scene in the first century, He revises that commandment with a twist. "A new command I give you: Love one another. As I have loved you, so you must love one another" (John 13:34).

As I have loved you. What does that mean? How did Jesus love us? With a cross.

189

But God demonstrates his own love for us in this: While we were still sinners, Christ died for us.

Romans 5:8

Jesus knows how it feels to be rejected. He knows how it feels to be insulted, humiliated, beaten down, and wrongly accused. If you can relate, then be encouraged—you're not alone. Jesus went before you.

He tells all of us, "Whoever wants to be my disciple must deny themselves and take up their cross daily and follow me" (Luke 9:23), and "if we are to share his glory, we must also share his suffering" (Romans 8:17 NLT). Sacrifice is part of the deal. We signed up for it the day we accepted Jesus as our Lord and Savior.

Yet don't lose the significance of those two words: Jesus is your *Lord* (He's in control, even when it doesn't feel like it), and He is your *Savior* (He ultimately saves you from the very worst pain, even when it doesn't feel like it). Every day that He keeps you here on this planet is a day He intends to grow your character until you are more and more like Him.

So this whole idea of blessing people who hurt you? Yep, that's one way to get the job done.

Not only that, but we rejoice in our sufferings, knowing that suffering produces endurance, and endurance produces character, and character produces hope, and hope does not put us to shame, because God's love has been poured into our hearts through the Holy Spirit who has been given to us.

Romans 5:3–5 ESV

How Can I Love Someone I Don't Even Like?

Before we can explore how to bless people who annoy us or hurt us, let me ask a question: *Why* don't you like them? Recall our discussions on perspective in chapters 9 and 10. Do you dislike someone because she's different from you? Do you find it hard to bless someone not because you can't but because you won't? Have you taken an interest in understanding this person, or are you stuck on your assumptions?

It could be that generous love only seems impossible because you're letting your biases get in the way. If that's the case, take a step back and gain the right perspective first. Then we can move on with a heart tuned to God.

Now. Some people are just hard to love, it's true. My friend Kristi spent years nursing a strained relationship with her mother, until one day while praying over this heartache she heard God say, *I love her, too.* "I realized then that God deems my mom worthy of unconditional love and grace and forgiveness," she said, "so I should, too."

Kristi started inviting her mom to dinner, showing more concern for her thoughts and preferences, hugging her, even calling to see if she needed anything while Kristi was out running errands. "This wasn't easy because we still had issues between us," Kristi said. But she prayed often for the peace of Christ to wash over her and not let the devil wheedle into her relationships.

> And "don't sin by letting anger control you." Don't let the sun go down while you are still angry, for anger gives a foothold to the devil.
>
> Ephesians 4:26–27 NLT

"All these things have aided in my heart transformation," Kristi said. "My heart is softened. I see my mom more through God's eyes versus my own human critical eyes. And I have seen a change in her heart, as well. She's more willing to help me out with my children, to serve us with family meals during the week when life gets crazy, and to share deeper thoughts and feelings."

Is their relationship perfect today? Not at all. But it's finally operating within the secure parameters of God's will and grace. Notice the progression of Kristi's obedience:

1. She prayed and sought God's truth.
2. She obeyed Him—one small step after another.
3. She experienced a change in her *own* heart (regardless of how her mother responded).

"God has been so gracious toward me and bears with me in all my shortcomings," she said. "For that reason I can bear with others and love them and forgive even if they don't ask for it. I can keep my own expectations in check and not place those on others. I am thankful for a loving, patient God, who does not keep a record of my wrongs or hold me to expectations that I cannot meet even if I tried. Blessing my mom has taught me to look through God's eyes and take the focus off self. Jesus is our best example of this, and may I always strive to be more like Him every day."

If You Think You're Not Getting Anywhere

Blessing people who don't respond can get old after a while. It's easy to give up. However, when we bless with the intent of doing it for God, we can keep going. And our actions gain greater purpose.

Therefore, my dear brothers and sisters, stand firm. Let nothing move you. Always give yourselves fully to the work of the Lord, because you know that your labor in the Lord is not in vain.

1 Corinthians 15:58

Still, don't you sometimes wish you could crack the nut, just a little bit? *Hey, grumpy person—give me a smile or a nod or a breath mint or something, just so I know I'm not talking to the wall here. Please?*

Ha. Maybe, just maybe, you have no idea the impact your blessings can make.

My friend Debbie arrived at her son's classroom after school one day to offer some last-minute help preparing for the school carnival.

The teacher had emailed saying they were short on volunteers and could use some extra hands. Debbie was available and happy to fill in, so she showed up. And she was greeted at the door by a fellow mom—a woman she'd never met—who took one look at Debbie and fired away.

"It's about time you got here!" the woman snarled. "I can't believe you volunteered for this and didn't bother to follow through!" Debbie stood shell-shocked as the woman went off on a five-minute tirade. When the ranting came to a pause, Debbie opened her mouth.

"I'm so sorry. You must think I'm someone else. I didn't sign up to help with coordinating this; I got a note from the teacher saying they needed extra help so I thought I could be useful."

"Well . . . then . . . you can go over there and work on that." The woman gave a brusque nod toward a project and quickly left the room. Debbie didn't see her again for the rest of the afternoon.

"There was no apology and no discussion after that," Debbie said. "I just worked on the task she gave me and went home."

How would you have responded to that situation? Would you have avoided the crotchety mom at all costs? Formed a nasty opinion about her? Glared at her in the hallway? Maybe you would've been tempted to talk about her with the other moms.

Sure. That's how most of the mothers in the school handled her. No one was friendly to this woman because she was friendly to no one.

But Debbie saw it differently.

"Something made her the way she is. When we encounter difficult people, we have to remember we don't know their story and what led them to being the way they are. I'm sure there's a background behind all those tougher personalities; there was something in this woman's past that made her gruff, that made her way of acting a defense mechanism. Our initial reaction is to repel those who repel us. But when the other moms mistreated this woman in return, it only expounded her attitude that the world was not a friendly place. God requires more from us than that—to love the unlovely."

After their initial meeting, Debbie would smile and say hello to the woman whenever she saw her. There was very little interaction between them other than crossing paths in the hall or in PTA meetings. The two women never built a real relationship; their children weren't even in the same grade. Yet this fellow mom was a constant presence in the school. "She was always stomping through the halls, frowning, as if she expected something was going to go wrong—she had that kind of negative attitude," Debbie said. "I was nothing more than kind and cordial with her even when her actions didn't warrant it."

After three years of this friendly/unfriendly synergy, Debbie's husband was relocated for work and the family prepared to move. The day the trucks arrived, her doorbell rang. There stood the grouchy school mom, holding a farewell gift. She reached out her arms and wrapped Debbie in a hug, weeping.

"I just heard the news," she sniffled. "I'm so sorry you're moving. I'm going to miss you so much!" Through free-flowing tears, she told Debbie how much she had enjoyed working with her at the school and how much her smiles had meant to her.

"I was just as shell-shocked at the end as I had been at the beginning. She was the last person I expected to see at my doorstep," Debbie said. "I had no idea she cared about me or appreciated me. She always gave me such a tough exterior. I just didn't respond with like behavior."

What does that tell us about the power of kindness? It breaks down barriers. It affects people in ways we may never know. It touches them with the love of Christ.

"It was totally God; it wasn't me," Debbie said. "When we live life, faithful to do those little things, God can work through that in the lives of others because it's not normal. Kindness isn't normal."

Why not? Why is genuine, God-led kindness so unusual in today's world? And what should we as Christians be doing to change that? Day after day, grouchy person upon grouchy person, each of us has the opportunity—the responsibility—to answer hate with love. God knows how vital this is to the kingdom. He commands it.

> But to you who are listening I say: Love your enemies, do good to those who hate you.
>
> Luke 6:27

Turn the Other What Now?

I need to pause here a moment and clarify a very important point. When it comes to being kind to the unkind, many of us misunderstand the Christian's role. Kindness in the face of cruelty is not a weakness. It's a strength—namely, *God's* strength—working in us.

> For it is God who works in you to will and to act in order to fulfill his good purpose.
>
> Philippians 2:13

Anyone can repay insult with insult. That's easy. But Jesus says Christians are called to take a higher road.

> "You have heard that it was said, 'Eye for eye, and tooth for tooth.' But I tell you, do not resist an evil person. If anyone slaps you on the right cheek, turn to them the other cheek also."
>
> Matthew 5:38–39

What does that mean? Christians are supposed to be punching bags? Nope. Not at all. This portion of Scripture is widely misunderstood. "Turning the other cheek" is not a passive act of resignation or defeat; it's actually a power move.

In Jesus' day, a Roman soldier would strike a subject's right cheek with the back of his right hand. This was meant to belittle the person being slapped. However, soldiers were forbidden to touch anyone

195

with their left hand because it was used for "dirty" functions and considered unclean. Therefore, when Jesus says to turn the other cheek, He is not telling His followers to cave; rather, He's calling them to a peaceful revolt. Forcing a soldier to strike your left cheek with his left hand would have been a disgrace to the soldier, as if to say, "You're determined to treat me as inferior—but I will take a stand for my equality."[1]

Blessing people who hurt you is an act of claiming your worth in Christ. Never let anyone convince you otherwise.

When Your Net Is Empty, Keep on Fishing

Are you weary, sweet sister? Tired of draining your heart trying to repair a broken relationship, blessing someone who never blesses you back? I get it. There's nothing like unrequited love to tear us apart inside. You give and you give and you give, and nothing ever changes.

Albert Einstein said the definition of insanity is doing the same thing over and over again and expecting different results. But I don't call that insanity.

I call it faith.

There's a story in the Gospel of Luke where Jesus is sitting in Simon Peter's boat speaking to a crowd along a lakeshore. When he finishes preaching, he tells Simon to put the boat out into deep water and let the nets down for a catch.

> Simon answered, "Master, we've worked hard all night and haven't caught anything. But because you say so, I will let down the nets."
>
> Luke 5:5

Can you just picture Simon rolling his eyes? *Oh, come on, Jesus. We already spent the entire night on this useless boat, and I'm telling you, the fish aren't biting. Been there, done that, ain't gonna happen.*

Again and again, Simon and his fishing buddies had tossed out their smelly old net with no results. Eventually they decided the fish had won this round, so they rowed back to shore—probably exhausted—and washed out their fishing gear. Time to go home and eat breakfast, right? So why does Simon drag his net back out? Because Jesus told him to.

And look what happens.

When they had done so, they caught such a large number of fish that their nets began to break. So they signaled their partners in the other boat to come and help them, and they came and filled both boats so full that they began to sink.

Luke 5:6–7

Are you kidding me?! Jesus didn't only give Simon what he hoped for—a net full of fish; He gave him *two boats* filled with fish. So many fish the poor boats couldn't handle the load!

Simon could've chosen to tell Jesus No—*there's no point in rowing out again.* But he didn't. He trusted Him even when the circumstances appeared fruitless. So Jesus rewarded Simon for his faith by giving him immeasurably more than he could ask or imagine (Ephesians 3:20).

What are you asking God for right now?

In your painful relationships, with those people in your life who take and never give—are you tossing out your net time after time with no results?

That's not insanity.

It's trust.

Because at any moment, God could decide—*today is the day. I'm going to fill your nets so full, your boat won't be big enough to carry all my blessings.* "For nothing is impossible with God" (Luke 1:37 ESV).

Do you want to know the most interesting part of this story? In the end, after Simon had caught the biggest haul of his life—a catch that probably could've earned him a month's or even a year's worth of wages—he chose to walk away from it all.

> Then Jesus said to Simon, "Don't be afraid; from now on you will catch men." So they pulled their boats up on shore, left everything and followed him.
>
> Luke 5:10–11

In our tough relationships, we think we're waiting for the big haul of fish—for a friend to beg forgiveness, for a prodigal child to return, for a broken marriage to be saved. We imagine that's the goal, the answer to so many hard-fought prayers.

But Jesus says, *not so.* He has something far more important in mind.

A chance to follow Him.

Maybe the purpose of your "insanity" is to draw you closer to your Savior. To discover how He fills your needs and knows everything you don't know. Whatever your challenge is, even as you get up tomorrow and face it all over again, will you trust Him? Will you believe that one day He's going to fill your net beyond capacity? Then maybe, just maybe, when that gift is in your hands, you'll realize it's nothing, really—compared to knowing the Giver.

Let's Dig Deeper

1. Read Isaiah 53:3–5. In what ways can Jesus relate to unrequited love and personal sacrifice? How does this passage impact your perspective on blessing others even when it's hard?

2. Read 1 Peter 3:9. Considering what we've explored in this chapter, why do you think Jesus calls us to repay evil with

blessing? What do you think it means that we may inherit a blessing as a result?

3. Mercy is one of God's core characteristics. Read the parable of the unmerciful servant in Matthew 18:21–35. How does mercy work to our advantage? Why should we extend it to others?

4. Proverbs 15:1 says, "A gentle answer turns away wrath, but a harsh word stirs up anger." How can you apply this truth to your interactions with the difficult people in your life?

5. Has God placed you in a leadership position? Read 2 Timothy 2:24. How are God's servants expected to treat others? How well are you doing in this area?

6. Think of a difficult relationship in your life. Can you see how God has been growing your character through it? Have you been cooperating or resisting God's work?

7. What would you have done in Debbie's situation? Have you had a similar experience? How did you react, and what was the result?

8. Before reading this chapter, what was your definition of "turn the other cheek"? Compare that to what we learned. What do you think of this command now?

Love in Motion

Review the steps Kristi took when she learned to bless her mother:

- Pray and seek God's truth (through Scripture)
- Obey Him—even if it's just in baby steps
- Discern a change in your own heart

Choose one difficult relationship in your life and start applying these principles. Keep a journal of prayers, pleas, praises, and results. Note how God works in this relationship over time.

— Chapter 16 —

About That Golden Rule

When I was growing up, my mother always taught me to treat others like I want to be treated. Yours too? Back then I thought it was Momma's wisdom; today I know it's called the Golden Rule, and it comes straight from the Bible.

So in everything, do to others what you would have them do to you, for this sums up the Law and the Prophets.

Matthew 7:12

I'd acknowledged this principle for over thirty years, but it had never really occurred to me how the Golden Rule applies to family life, until the day my daughter broke the rule.

"Mom, you should *not* have done this!" My firstborn, age five at the time, stormed into the bathroom where I stood threading silver hoops into my earlobes. She glared at me, her lips pursed and a fist perched on each hip.

"Pardon me?" I turned from the mirror to face her. "What exactly did I do?"

"You left the car door open all night!" she hissed. "Dad just went into the garage and saw it!"

Oh. I did? My brain rewound to the night before—a family dinner outing to Applebee's. I recalled unloading two kids, two water cups, a bulky purse, and a Styrofoam to-go box from the minivan, so it's entirely possible my juggling fingers forgot to push the button on the automatic sliding door. Sure, that sounds like something I would do.

"Well, I'm sorry. I'm human, and I make mistakes." Annoyed, I held my accuser's stare. "And I don't appreciate your tone, young lady. How would you feel if I scolded you every time you made a mistake?"

Whoa. A revelation flickered in my head and cut my lecture short. I *do* scold her for making mistakes.

How many times have I reacted to harmless errors with impatience instead of grace? I'm ashamed of the examples. Can you relate to any of these?

Me: Who took the masking tape?

Daughter: I'm sorry, Mom. I used it for a craft, and I forgot to put it back in the junk drawer.

Me: No more masking tape for you.

What I wish I'd said: We can all be forgetful sometimes. I'll help you look for it.

Me: Ouch! You just kicked me in the shin!

Daughter: I'm sorry, Mom. I was practicing my karate.

Me: Go practice somewhere else.

What I wish I'd said: The kitchen is too small for roundhouse kicks. Let's go in the playroom so you can show me your fancy moves.

Me: Okay, it's time to add the cinnamon.

Daughter: Here it is, Mom!

Me: Aaack! You just poured cumin into our cookie batter! Now we have to start all over.

What I wish I'd said: Spicy cookies coming right up! (Insert crazy peals of laughter.)

When my daughter harped on me for the car door blunder, I heard my own criticism in her sassy mouth. If I expect my kids to cut their poor mother some slack, then I must set the example first. More kindness. More forgiveness. More grace.

In other words, less me—and more Jesus. After all, how can any of us *give* grace unless we *receive* it from Him first?

> Always be humble and gentle. Be patient with each other, making allowance for each other's faults because of your love.
>
> Ephesians 4:2 NLT

Grace is a necessary ingredient in generous love. It's not an optional add-in or the frosting on top. It is absolutely integral to the recipe. Why? Because grace is how we live out the Golden Rule. Treat others how we would want to be treated—even when they don't deserve it.

How I Saw Jesus in a Hairbrush

"If you think of it, can you bring my *Redeeming Love* book to Bible study tomorrow? Thanks!"

I stared at this text from my friend Karyn and felt a burning sensation creep into my cheeks. *I still have that book?! Didn't she lend me that, like, two years ago? No way—please tell me I gave it back.*

So I tripped downstairs to the bookshelf. Sure enough, there it was, *Redeeming Love*, stacked on top of a pile of novels. Worse yet, I found three other hijacked books whose rightful owners must be cursing my name.

And that's not all.

My TV cabinet still holds a DVD lent to me in 2009.

My sister's maternity jacket lives in my closet. I kept it through my last pregnancy—and hers.

Twice a year, our local library pardons overdue fines if we donate nonperishable goods. I mark this event on my calendar and clip every cereal coupon I can find.

Once, somebody lent me a paintbrush and I lost it. My husband found it stashed in an empty suitcase six months later. Don't ask me how it got there. I'm still stumped.

Ugh! I don't want to be a thief. I just can't seem to get it together in this area. I'm a horrible borrower, okay? I used to berate myself for it, but over the years I've accepted this flaw, and now for the sake of all parties involved I'll politely refuse whenever anyone offers to lend me anything. Really, it's for the best. You need your can opener more than I do.

Yet understand this: yes, I am a terrible borrower—but that does not make me a terrible friend.

I might hoard your things, but I won't neglect your heart. I'll handle your thoughts, your hopes, and your dreams with care. I'll share your laughter and your sadness. I'll treat you the way you want to be treated.

Because this little borrowing flaw of mine? It does not own me. None of my flaws can.

Only God gets that job.

He saved us, not because of righteous things we had done, but because of his mercy. He saved us through the washing of rebirth and renewal by the Holy Spirit, whom he poured out on us generously through Jesus Christ our Savior, so that, having been justified by his grace, we might become heirs having the hope of eternal life.

Titus 3:5–7

Do you have some quirks you can't shake? Do you beat yourself up over shortcomings or social blunders? Do you feel like no matter how hard you try to bless others, you just keep messing it up?

Maybe you're the friend who's always late. Or you're notorious for saying the wrong thing at the wrong time. Maybe you forget birthdays, dinner plans, or names.

So what? I've said it before, and I'll say it again and again—not a single one of us is perfect, and yet God chooses to love us. He chooses to bless us. We can do the same for each other.

Karyn did.

I met her at the doors to Bible study a few days after her text, with my eyes to the carpet and her book in my guilty hands. She laughed and pulled a gift from her purse—a Wet Brush for my daughters, just like the one belonging to her own daughter, which I'd admired the last time we visited. Of course she didn't offer to lend me hers, smart woman. This brush was brand-spanking-new, still in the packaging.

Imagine that. I messed up, and my friend responded by giving me a gift I don't deserve.

Who does that sound like?

Jesus showers us with His ongoing mercy and grace. What a privilege we have to extend it to others. How can you show grace to your friends today? To your children, your husband, your neighbors—even strangers? Show me a person who's breathing and I'll show you someone in desperate need of grace. As believers, we're called to spread it. And that is one of the greatest blessings we can possibly give or receive.

> And now I entrust you to God and the message of his grace that is able to build you up and give you an inheritance with all those he has set apart for himself.
>
> Acts 20:32 NLT

Watch Your Language

This might come as a shock, but I need to point out that nobody else is you.

Huh?

It's true. Your child is not you. Your spouse, your friends, your co-workers, your church group, your mail carrier for goodness' sake—anyone and everyone in the universe who is not you (which is everyone besides you)—they are not you.

Umm, duh?

Yes, we think we know that already, but do we *act* like we know? Very often the only obstacle between you and the ability to bless someone you care about is the basic acknowledgement that the other person is an individual, with tastes and desires that may be different from your own.

It's called their love language. You have one, too.

Maybe you've heard of pastor Gary Chapman's love languages phenomenon, and maybe you've even taken a quiz to determine your own love language.[1] The idea is that if you show love to another person in the way that best expresses love to them (i.e., their love language), you'll achieve maximum results in blessing that person. The five options are:

- Words of affirmation (that's mine)
- Acts of service
- Receiving gifts
- Quality time
- Physical touch

For example, my younger daughter's love language is definitely receiving gifts. This girl flies over Jupiter for a chance to visit the Dollar Store and pick out a toy or gadget. She has come home with ninja masks, Hawaiian skirts, make-your-own-airplane kits, and most recently a pink stuffed snake. You never know what you'll find at the Dollar Store.

Yet my preferred love language is gushy words. Like when we're driving home from the Dollar Store and my daughter tells me I'm the best mom ever-ever-ever in the whole wide world because I bought her a pink snake. Ooh, I melt. I feel blessed!

206

So what happens if I attempt to bless her back using nothing but gushy words? She appreciates them, sure, but they don't trip her blessing trigger quite like a new pack of Legos. Or another stuffed snake. (That's my girl.)

The trouble is, many of us still default to blessing other people the way we would want to be blessed. I mean, that's the Golden Rule, right? Well, sort of. It seems counterintuitive, but in order to treat someone the way you want to be treated, you first need to understand that they may not want to be treated quite the same way you want to be treated.

Say what?

Let's put it this way. The overarching rule is to love others. But *how* you love them makes all the difference. If we speak to our loved ones according to our own love language and not theirs, we'll miss out on a chance to bless them to the max. So use whatever love language speaks loudest to the person in front of you. Not sure what that is? Go to 5lovelanguages.com and take the quiz.

What Does Your Behavior Say About You?

If we truly live according to the Golden Rule, treating people the way we want to be treated, then how we behave toward others should reveal something about us, such as:

- I respect my husband's opinions; I want him to respect mine.
- I keep a friend's confidence; I want to trust her with my own.
- I pray for people who are hurting, because when my turn comes, it will bless me to know others are lifting me up in prayer.

Sounds like a perfect formula, right? Imagine if the world actually worked that way! If in our homes, schools, workplaces, churches, and communities everyone was assured kindness and support simply because the people around us desire kindness and support. What a beautiful cycle.

Too bad it's broken.

We all know that nobody follows the Golden Rule completely—you and me included. Unless I somehow wish to be scolded for tracking wet shoes into the house, I'm pretty sure I'm not a shining example of the Golden Rule in action.

But once again, the trouble with our interpretation of the Golden Rule is selfishness. It presupposes a focus on self—treat others how I would want to be treated; love them the way I would want to be loved.

What if the rule is actually for a higher purpose beyond ourselves? It is.

No one has ever seen God; but if we love one another, God lives in us and his love is made complete in us.

1 John 4:12

Ultimately, our kindness, blessing, and love toward others are gifts we offer to God. They complete the love He first gave to us. They make our invisible Creator known! And—a really cool bonus because our God is just that awesome—He then uses these gifts as tools within our own lives to protect us, heal us, and bless us in return.

Above all, love each other deeply, because love covers over a multitude of sins.

1 Peter 4:8

Bottom line—why does the Golden Rule exist? Because loving others is the mark of a true Christian (John 13:35). Every interaction with another human being is an opportunity to share the love of Christ. We are His voice, His hands, and His face on earth. What an amazing privilege. Let's use it for His glory, amen?

Let Them Bless You

Finally, sisters, I'd like to share some thoughts with those of you who struggle not with giving blessings, necessarily, but with receiving them. You know who you are.

I'm thinking of my friends who flinch at every compliment. The women who refuse gifts and help of any sort, or else feel guilty, unworthy, or embarrassed when coerced to accept.

Are you afraid to ask for prayer?

Determined to handle every challenge by yourself?

Do you mistakenly believe that having a need means you are somehow flawed?

Ah. Well then you need to meet my friend Sara.

She's a mother of three—an attorney by trade. She's sharp. She has a brain.

And she also has a fear—of being home alone.

This is a lifelong phobia, rooted in her since childhood. Whenever her husband leaves overnight on business, Sara battles a crippling anxiety that overtakes her sensibilities.

"I feel like I shouldn't have this fear," she said. "I'm an adult; I should be able to handle being home with my children when my husband is gone. But I hear every noise, my heart pounds, I can't sleep. At one point in my life it was completely debilitating and terrifying."

For years, Sara kept her fear private. She presumed people would think she was crazy if they knew. Finally, though, she reached out to a trusted friend and admitted her struggle.

"Emily immediately responded to say she was praying," Sara said. "And from then on—to this day—she took my need and made it her own."

First Emily assured Sara she was not crazy. She validated her fears by confessing she had fears, too. At night, when Emily was up nursing babies, she prayed for Sara and sent her texts and Bible verses and tips on how to proclaim God's truths over her household.

Emily was compassionate. She was kind. She loved generously. And through her blessing, God began to break the stronghold in Sara's life. "God used Emily's support to release me from this burden," Sara said. "I still struggle, but now God gives me peace when I focus on His commands to think about things that are true and lovely. I meditate on the points Emily and I talked about, that God made everything—the darkness and night, too, and He knows everything, He never tires, never sleeps, and therefore I have to trust. And I do. My trust in Him has grown. I can finally sleep through the night."

> In peace I will lie down and sleep, for you alone, Lord, make me dwell in safety.
>
> Psalm 4:8

God uses our blessings—for our benefit, for other people's benefit, and ultimately for His glory. So don't deny someone the opportunity to bless and be blessed. Humbly accept their blessing. Sometimes that is the most generous act of love there is.

> The one who blesses others is abundantly blessed; those who help others are helped.
>
> Proverbs 11:25 THE MESSAGE

———— Let's Dig Deeper ————

1. In your own words, recite the Golden Rule. How well are you following this rule in your family lately? How about in your church, neighborhood, workplace, etc.?

2. Fill in the blanks: *It is important to me that* _____ *[my husband, my children, my boss, etc.] treat(s) me with* _____ *[love, honesty, respect, gentleness, etc.].* Are you treating them likewise?.

3. Do you make allowance for other people's faults, especially those of your family and friends? Or do you criticize more readily than you forgive? (See Ephesians 4:2–3.)

4. Grace means to get something good that we do not deserve. It is unmerited favor. God gives it to us, His children, and out of our gratitude we ought to feel compelled to extend grace to others in the form of blessings. This is easier for some people than others. Does extending grace come naturally to you? Or are you more likely to expect people to earn your favor?

5. Think of the last time a friend irked you. How did you respond? How could you have blessed your friend in that situation?

6. Now think of the last time *you* irked someone else. How did they respond? How did that make you feel?

7. Have you been treating others as though they're you? As if they desire and appreciate the same things you do, even if that's not true? If so, how might you be missing opportunities to bless them?

8. How can the Golden Rule actually cause us to think selfishly?

Love in Motion

Go to 5lovelanguages.com and take the love language quiz. Encourage your husband and children to complete the quiz, too (or take the quiz on behalf of your little kids). Even if you've taken the quiz before, I encourage you to take it again. As seasons change, our needs may change; therefore, our love languages may evolve, as well.

Did anything surprise you in the quiz results? Did they give you a better understanding of how to bless your loved ones? Choose one action this week that speaks to each of your household members in their love language.

— Epilogue —

A Life Well-Lived

I imagine heaven is filled with fishing boats. If we could catch a glimpse right now, we'd see a redheaded dad casting a line into the pristine water, standing tall beside his sweet daughter whose lovely blond hair glows like the rising sun. They are smiling, laughing, filled with unspeakable joy.

They are not dead. They are fully alive.

As I type these words, it is exactly two years from the day Jesus called them home—Jon and Olivia, Erin's beloveds, two devoted children of God. Those of us left here remain staunchly convinced God has a reason for this, for two empty seats at the table every morning and every night, for the heartache that will never really go away this side of heaven. Erin believes God is good. She inspires me to agree.

Even in her grief, Erin knows her husband's heart. He would not want her to doubt her faith through this suffering. He would want her to hold fast to the only One who loves her even more than he did.

Oh, how Jon loved her.

When they met, Erin was a new believer. Jon was the goofy kid in youth group who joked about everything—except for his faith. From a young age, he truly wanted to know God. Jon chose God first, even over his relationship with Erin when he moved across the country to attend Bible college before they were married. God was always foremost in Jon's life. And how did he show it?

By loving other people.

"He was the fellowship junkie," Erin described. "He wanted to be involved in every church event, he wanted to serve people any way he could. He even made sure he sat in a different seat every Sunday morning at church just so he could meet and talk with someone new."

Jon served his family first. He encouraged his wife with the Word. He carved out time to help his children with math homework, to teach them how to run the snow blower, to read to them every night for an hour, straight from the Bible. He loved hosting guests for meals despite the family's snug kitchen. Friends and neighbors knew Jon as the go-to man for helping load moving trucks or cut down trees. He openly read his Bible at work and welcomed questions from co-workers. He called loved ones just to keep in touch.

Jon loved others with his presence.

He led his family to save money for a kingdom fund, which they used to support missions. They tithed their tax return to a new ministry every year. And when it came time to replace a car, Jon rarely sold the old one; he gave it away to someone in need.

Jon loved others with his possessions.

People were drawn to Jon. He made friends easily, from every walk of life—every background, every color, every shape, and every size. He didn't care what a person looked like or where they came from. He offered his authentic friendship, free of judgment and filled with genuine interest in knowing another soul.

Jon loved others with his perspective.

And this man after God's own heart, this faithful son of the King, he *knew* how to pray. It was part of his lifestyle, his constant communication with the Father. He prayed for and with his family. He lifted others up to the Lord. Friends quickly learned that if they were especially hungry, they'd better not assign Jon the job of saying grace, because the food would get cold long before his prayer was done.

Jon loved others with his prayers.

This godly man was given only thirty-three years. But during that time—the very same lifespan as Jesus himself—Jon made a lasting impact. He built a legacy. He lived an abundant life.

He reflected the glory of the Lord.

Not because he was perfect or glamorous.

Not because he made a ton of money or traveled the globe.

Not because he earned high credentials or a shelf of worldly accolades.

Not because he was the most talented or most athletic or most likely to succeed at everything.

None of that matters in the end.

So what does, really?

What is the true measure of a life well-lived?

Love.

And Jon did that very, very well.

A new command I give you: Love one another. As I have loved you, so you must love one another. By this everyone will know that you are my disciples, if you love one another.

John 13:34–35

How do you want to be remembered someday? You can choose right now who you want to be tomorrow—who your friends and family and your children's children's children will remember long after you part from this earth.

You can choose this moment who you will be *today*, to the people living in your home and working at your office and driving through your neighborhood streets.

215

You can choose—yes or no—to be an ambassador for Christ, right where you are.

It's up to you.

Will you look beyond yourself toward others?

Will you shine your precious star for a darkened world to see?

Will you dare to make a difference for eternity?

Then join the revolution, my friends. Let's do it together.

Love—generously.

It really is as simple, as powerful, and as beautiful as that.

Bonus Materials

For a collection of supplementary resources available to download, including blessing cards, prayer journals, keychain verses, and more, visit www.beckykopitzke.com/generouslove.

Acknowledgments

To Erin, my beautiful friend. Thank you for planting the seed that flourished into *Generous Love*. I'm so grateful for your willingness to share your story, your open heart, and your love for Jesus. May He be glorified above all.

To Chad, the one God gave me. In my heart, I want to bless you most. Thank you for loving me even when I fail. I treasure your support.

To my chickadees. You bless me more than you will ever know. Thank you for being my very best cheerleaders. Mom loves you.

To my prayer warriors. Thank you for lifting me up throughout the creation of this book. You did the important work, and I'm so very grateful.

To Judy Episcopo, Heidi Scott, and Kate Schwarzenbart. You've been my extra eyes, my checkpoints, and my wise counselors. Thank you for your insight and encouragement.

To my agent, Blythe Daniel. Thank you for believing in me and prayerfully opening the doors.

To Kim Bangs. You opened my eyes to what this book was meant to become. Thank you for stretching me, supporting me, and challenging me to dream.

To the entire team at Bethany House. Thank you for championing *Generous Love* and bringing it so beautifully to life.

To Tammy Muller, my mentor and friend. Some of my favorite hours are spent sipping coffee and discussing theology with you. Thank you for pouring into me.

To Amber, my iron that sharpens iron. You keep me humble. Thank you for your unconditional friendship.

To my circle of friends and "family" at AAC and FVCA. Thank you for doing life with the Kopitzkes. God has blessed us with your love and support.

To my Facebook friends. Thank you for answering every call for ideas and experiences. You truly helped to shape this book.

To every person who invited me to share their stories. Thank you for offering your heartfelt transparency and your desire to make God known.

To you, the reader holding this book. Thank you dearly for spending these pages with me. I pray the words written here will inspire you to demonstrate generous love for Christ's glory.

Above all, thank you, Jesus—for everything.

Notes

Chapter 1: What Is a Blessing, Anyway?

1. "Why Do We Say 'God Bless You' When Someone Sneezes?" Got Questions Ministries, accessed May 19, 2016, http://www.gotquestions.org/God-bless-you-sneeze.html.

2. John Piper, "God Is Always Doing 10,000 Things in Your Life," Desiring God, January 1, 2013, accessed April 29, 2017, www.desiringgod.org/articles/every-moment-in-2013-god-will-be-doing-10-000-things-in-your-life.

Chapter 3: The "Me" Weeds

1. Rick Warren, "The Four Laws of God's Blessing," Pastor Rick's Daily Hope, May 21, 2014, accessed May 26, 2016,. http://rickwarren.org/devotional/english/the-four-laws-of-god-s-blessing_814.

Chapter 11: Four P's of Blessing—#4 Prayer

1. Adrian Rogers, "The Privilege of Prayer," Christianity.com, accessed April 8, 2017, http://www.christianity.com/christian-life/prayer/the-privilege-of-prayer-11549313.html.

2. "Pray About Little Things," Bible Hub, accessed April 8, 2017, http://biblehub.com/sermons/pub/pray_about_little_things.htm.

Chapter 15: When Blessing Is Hard

1. David P. Gushee and Glen H. Stassen, *Kingdom Ethics: Following Jesus in Contemporary Context* (Downers Grove, IL: InterVarsity Press, 2003).

Chapter 16: About That Golden Rule

1. Gary Chapman, *The 5 Love Languages* (Chicago: Northfield, 2015).

—— About the Author ——

Becky Kopitzke is a writer, speaker, mentor, dreamer, believer, lunch packer, and recovering perfectionist. She and her husband, Chad, live in northeast Wisconsin with their two lovely daughters and a tank full of guppies. Plus, at long last, a dog.

When she's not writing, Becky can be found volunteering at school, leading Bible studies, singing on the worship team, neglecting the laundry, mediating sibling squabbles, and attempting to engage in adult conversation with her husband while the children beg for marshmallows. It's an ordinary, magnificent, crumbs-on-the-kitchen-floor life. She calls it *blessed*.

Connect with Becky on her website, www.beckykopitzke.com.